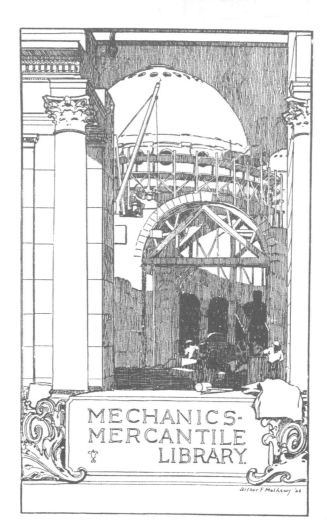

MECHANICS-
MERCANTILE
LIBRARY.

Arthur F. Mathews '06

INSURMOUNTABLE SIMPLICITIES

Insurmountable Simplicities

39 PHILOSOPHICAL CONUNDRUMS

ROBERTO CASATI + ACHILLE VARZI

TRANSLATED BY *ACHILLE VARZI*

COLUMBIA UNIVERSITY PRESS   NEW YORK

COLUMBIA UNIVERSITY PRESS

Publishers Since 1893
New York   Chichester, West Sussex

Copyright © 2004 Gius. Laterza & Figli, Roma-Bari
Translation copyright © 2006 Columbia University Press
All rights reserved

Library of Congress Cataloging-in-Publication Data

Casati, Roberto, 1961–
    [Semplicitá insormontabili English]
    Insurmountable simplicities : thirty-nine philosophical stories /
Roberto Casati, Achille C. Varzi.
        p. cm.
    Includes bibliographical references and index.
    ISBN 0–231–13722–2 (alk. paper)
    I. Varzi, Achille C.   II. Title.

PQ4863.A7768S4613 2006
853'.92—dc22
                                                        2005031592

♾ Columbia University Press books are printed on
permanent and durable acid-free paper.

Printed in the United States of America

C 10 9 8 7 6 5 4 3 2 1

CONTENTS

INSURMOUNTABLE SIMPLICITIES

Perhaps not all the stories that follow are true. They could, however, be true, and the Reader is invited to ponder this. Should she reckon that things are otherwise—that some of the stories lack the gift not only of Verity, but also of Possibility—we would not insist. But for the time being, let us simply proceed to introduce chapter

1

in which the first character immediately vanishes after solving in his own way a paralyzing enigma concerning the Reason of things and human Freedom, and in which notable metaphysical problems concerning Cause and Time are addressed, including whether it is reasonable to build a machine to travel back into the Past, and whether, by traveling back into the Past, one could induce changes in the Present; and in which at last our two main characters make their entrance to propose an incontrovertible amendment of the Laws—if such there be—of a top-scorer List.

ROOM 88

"Hi Sarah, it's me. Just a quick message to let you know that I got here all right. The hotel is fine. The room is spacious and well furnished, and there is a lot of light—you would like it. There's just a funny echo effect (I can hear my own voice), but I can live with that. I'm going to take a shower, then I'll go out for a walk to explore the neighborhood. Coming from the airport I already had a chance to see the park and the beach that opens onto the ocean. Looks beautiful. Give me a call when you get back!"

"Hi Sarah, it's me again. You should see the mirror in this room. It's huge. It fills an entire wall, right across from the window, and it makes the room look even brighter and wider. That's how you thought we should renovate our study, right? Well, I would say it now seems like a great idea: this room *really* looks twice as big. We'll talk about it later, OK?"

"Sarah, where are you? Did you get my messages? I haven't gone out yet; I guess it's better if I take a nap first. This big mirror is unbeliev-able—you should see it. I wonder how they managed to bring it into the room; it certainly couldn't go through the door. Perhaps they put it up as they were building the room . . . It's mounted directly on the wall, with no visible support, and its surface is perfectly clean, with no trace of smudge or silver cast. The images are so clear they seem real. Do you think we can find something similar back home? Please call me when you get back."

"Sorry, me again. I hope I'm not clogging up your voice mail. Unfortu-nately, I couldn't rest. This mirror makes me nervous. I looked at it closely: it is simply perfect. Not only that. I've touched it more than once but I didn't leave any fingerprints. If you touch a glass surface you always leave a mark, right? Well, in this case it is as though I didn't even get close to it. What can it be made of? I even tried to scratch it—no way. Something else is strange: you can't write on this mirror. I tried with a thick felt-tip pen. Nothing at all!"

"Hello Sarah? Now you are going to say I am crazy, but I am beginning to think that this might not even *be* a mirror. There are no mirrors like this. I am beginning to suspect that there is nothing at all there, and that what I see in the "mirror" is actually real. It is as though there were a plane dividing the room into two absolutely symmetrical halves. The problem is that I can't go over to the other side and check, because I keep running into my own image. Or rather, I don't quite know how to put this, but I am afraid that it's not my image at all. I'm afraid it's someone else who looks exactly like me and moves exactly like me. What sort of joke is this?"

"Sarah? Sarah? It feels *warm* to the touch!"

"Why aren't you returning my calls? I am really worried. I have tried and tried, but no way: this guy makes exactly the same movements I make. He copies everything I do. The only difference is that he parts his hair on the other side and he prefers to use his left hand. Is his heart in the right place?"

"I need to talk to you. I've been here for four hours but it feels like eternity. Or perhaps I should say *we* have been here for four hours. It's obvious that there are two of us. And perhaps there are two of you, too. Otherwise whom is he calling this very moment? I am sure we not only look and move alike—we must be thinking the same thoughts too, and have the same worries. Sarah, don't laugh, but I am starting to think that this 'mirror' is a sort of boundary between our universe and its own perfect replica. I'm going out now to check whether the symmetry continues outside or is just an aberration of this room."

"Me again. I didn't go out—I didn't dare. At least in here I have the feeling of being in charge of the situation. I can control *all* of his movements. He is just like a puppet I can move as I wish, if you know what I mean."

"Hold on—perhaps I'm not the controller, but the one being controlled? Perhaps *I'm* the puppet? But I don't feel controlled. I feel completely free to do what I want, like always. I decide whether to raise my arm. I decide whether to call you and leave you all these messages. I decide to turn around, if I wish. Perhaps we are both free and controlled at the same time? Please, Sarah, call me as soon as you get back!"

"Where are you, Sarah? I must do something. I have to get rid of this guy, but I just don't have the faintest idea how to do that. I tried leaving the room and then coming back in, but of course he did the same thing."

"He has a gun just like mine. I have been trying not to think that I want to shoot him, because I thought that way he wouldn't think of shooting me either. But nothing would happen anyway, right? Our bullets would collide right there in the middle of the room, and drop to the floor. Sarah call me—this is a nightmare."

"Sarah? There is a way I could get rid of him—just one way."

ABOUT A USELESS PROJECT

DEAR REVIEW COMMITTEE:

It is not our practice to raise complaints against a negative review report. We believe in peer refereeing and we respect it, whatever its content and consequences. However, in the case of our latest grant application (the "Time Machine" project), we cannot help but express our astonishment at the reasons given for your turning down our request for funding. Your main objection appears to be that our project is "philosophically interesting" but "useless in practice," by which you mean that the project "has no potential for application." We do not really think that the main criterion for judging the scientific value of a project should be its practical usefulness, but never mind that. Let us agree that usefulness is a relevant criterion, especially when large amounts of money are involved. Why should that be a reason to turn down our project? Quite frankly, we cannot think of a project with better application potential than ours. Some examples:

- *Cultural tourism*: One could send hordes of history fans back in time to witness the crucial episodes of the French Revolution, or to watch the Egyptians build the pyramids, or to videotape Socrates' lectures.

- *Exotic safaris*: We have already received several applications for
  dinosaur-hunting expeditions (why not, since they died off anyway?).
- *Error detection*: We could take a closer look at our past mistakes and
  learn how to avoid them in the future.
- *Historic documentaries*: Think of the huge saving in set design,
  costumes, special effects, etc. (How much did *Gladiator* cost?)

And so on and so forth. Honestly, can you think of a project with better
prospects for useful and thrilling applications?

Sincerely yours,
The "Time Machine" Research Group

DEAR "TIME MACHINE" RESEARCH GROUP:

Thank you for your letter. We agree that it would be interesting to
exploit a time machine for the uses that you suggest. It would also be
desirable if we could use it to prevent all sorts of unpleasant events that
happened in the past. It would be desirable, for instance, to be able to
go back to November 22, 1963, and prevent Lee Harvey Oswald from
killing John Kennedy, or to go back to April 14, 1912, and steer the Ti-
tanic around the iceberg. It would be excellent indeed to be able to do
such things. However, suppose your project were successful. Suppose
you *do* manage to build a time machine. Then why *didn't* you do any of
those things? Why is it that our past history is still full of such disas-
trous events? *Either* this means that your project is doomed to fail and
you will never manage to build a time machine, *or else* it means that the
project will succeed but that you are not going to use your time machine
for those beneficial purposes. In the first case, logic shows it would be
pointless to support your project. In the second case, ethics dictates that it
would be wrong to do so. Either way, you must concede that the reasons
against your project are overwhelming.

Cordially yours,
The Review Committee

DEAR REVIEW COMMITTEE:

Of course you noticed that our suggestions for practical applications of the time machine did not include any uses that would result in an alteration of the natural course of history. As a matter of fact, we believe that no such alteration is logically possible. According to our project, it is logically possible to *visit* the past but not to *modify* the past. No time traveler can undo what has been done or do what has not been done. So the logic is safe. This does not mean that the time traveler will be ineffectual during her stay in the past, of course; it simply means that what she is going to do is something she has already done. An accurate catalogue of all past events would include an account of the arrival of the Time Machine from out of nothing as well as an account of all the actions and reactions that followed. And ethics is safe too. For, if indeed we did manage to go back to Dallas, we could not stop Oswald from doing what he did. Nobody would be able to stop Oswald because nobody was able to stop him (and nobody was able to stop Oswald because nobody will ever be able to do so, even if they came from the future). Alas, the past is full of somber events, but there is nothing that we can do about that.

Respectfully yours,
The "Time Machine" Research Group

DEAR "TIME MACHINE" RESEARCH GROUP:

We appreciate the distinction between changing the past (impossible) and affecting the past (possible). However, this simply reinforces our initial impression: your project has no practical value. If in order to travel to the past one has to have been there already, and if one can only do what has already been done, then *à quoi bon l'effort?* Why should we invest in a "Time Machine" at all? We are afraid that our decision is now final.

Yours with best wishes,
The Review Committee

THE POET AS A YOUNG MAN

The career of Z., possibly the greatest poet of the twentieth century, has hitherto constituted a genuine puzzle. Critics and historians alike have never been able to explain how a person who spent his adolescence and the first years of his young adulthood living in an aimless manner should suddenly change his lifestyle and devote himself to the stanzas that made him so famous. Nobody could ever explain how the Z. whom many describe as a shy bookkeeper could be the same Z. whose verses are today among the most frequently reprinted of all time. We believe we are finally in a position to produce a document that may shed light on this puzzle. It is a letter autographed by Z. himself and dated May 8, 1937, just a few days before what is unanimously considered the date of the first authentic composition by the great poet. We reproduce it here in its entirety, with only a few editorial adjustments.

My dearest Lena,

[*Omissis*] . . . the man shows up at the door early this morning, when I am still in bed. Mrs. Lipschytz [the landlady] must have let him in. He says his name is [unreadable word]. He wears unusual clothes and speaks in a strange way: he is certainly not from around here. He says he comes from the future, from the twenty-third century.

"From the future?" I ask, while I quickly button my shirt and pull my pants on. He explains that he traveled in a time machine, which is apparently a vehicle that can move back and forth along the span of the years, the way an ordinary car takes us from one place to another. He claims that in his world, he is an esteemed literary scholar and that he has written many books, including some that he is carrying in his briefcase. He says that he devoted twenty years of his life to *my* work, and that he is greatly honored to meet me personally at last.

I give him a chair and begin to clean up the table, as he seems a bit uneasy. "Sorry about the mess," I say. He gives me a little smile and then goes on talking, while his eyes roam around, inspecting my room. "I have come for an interview," he says. "In my time you are considered the greatest of the literary classics. Your poems are a peerless model of style and creativity." Poems? He continues: "The school where I studied is named after you. Streets and avenues around the world celebrate your fame. Old and young know your verses by heart and declaim them with deep feeling. I am most greatly honored." I really don't understand what he is talking about. "I took the liberty of bringing some monographs that I have devoted to your work, especially to your early years. And I also brought a copy of the critical edition of your *Opera Omnia*, edited by me."

I try to say something but he continues: "If you don't mind, I would greatly appreciate it if you could show me your personal library. One of the main gaps in our knowledge, which your biographers could never fill, concerns precisely this aspect of your education. At the moment, you are twenty years old, correct? As far as we know, none of the books you now own have survived. Would you be so kind as to tell me—who are your favorite authors, what are your most beloved works?" I show him my books. The authors don't seem to mean much to him. He takes some notes but looks disappointed. "You *must* have some ideal teachers, some writers who inspired your style in some way. It is specifically to shed light on this aspect of your career that I came to visit you. I hope you won't find this too intrusive: every other means of research proved fruitless." I tell him that I don't mind at all, on the contrary—but he must be looking for someone else. At this point, however, he opens one of his books and reads some passages about things that actually did happen to me and to my brothers some years ago. He also shows me some pictures, and they are surely of me. There's even a photograph of me wearing the pants and the shirt that I am wearing at that very moment, sitting at the table with a book open in front of me. I raise my eyes to ask who took that picture and a blinding light dazzles me. "Please excuse the flash," says he, as he puts the strange device from which the light came back into his briefcase.

As I make coffee, he gets up and begins to look around, rummaging through the mess. "May I have a look at the other rooms? You know, I have very little time and I would like to collect as much material as possible." I kindly ask him to explain what this is all about, but he continues. "I embarked in a very complicated trip to come and see you. If you could at least show me some note, a draft of some sort, a poem that you keep in your drawers. So many readers would be delighted at the discovery of some unpublished works of yours." Of course I only have some notes of no significance, but I show them to him anyway. I also give him the short ballad that I wrote for your birthday. He reads it silently and gives it back to me without saying a word.

He seems to be in a rush. He is visibly impatient. Then he suddenly gets up and leaves the room in a hurry without even saying good-bye. Strange character indeed. The fact is, he forgot his briefcase. And his books, too. I started browsing through them and they are quite remarkable. They are all about me, or at least about someone with my name. They say that at a certain point I started to write wonderful lyrics. I have read some of them and I must say they are very intense and moving. Am I supposed to be their author? Did I really compose these lines?

Lena, I have thought a lot about this, after my guest left. If that is what *they* say, and if that is *I*, then that is what happened—isn't it? Or rather, that is what will happen. If indeed I wrote all of those poems, then it means that I will write them. Here it says that I will live a long life, so I have plenty of time at my disposal. Nor am I short of ink and paper. What I don't understand is *how* I can write poems that read as beautifully as the ones I have found in my *Opera Omnia*. Look, let me copy out the first one in full, so you can see for yourself . . .

THE CHAIN OF EVENTS
LEADING UP TO THE GOAL

HE, *closing the newspaper*. I always had problems with the top-scorer lists in soccer. I find them unfair, if not untruthful. Andy steals the ball and steamrolls down the field, dribbles around five opponents, survives a heavy shoulder charge, turns around heroically, and from an impossible position, blasts an amazing grass-clipping shot. The ball goes in the net, but only after a slight, accidental deflection by Bill, a fullback from the other team.

SHE. So it's counted as an "own goal."

HE. Exactly: the top-scorer list doesn't change, and the event goes into the record book as an error by Bill. A few minutes later, Andy dribbles past a series of opponents on the outer wing, is tripped shamelessly, gets up again, and blasts a brilliant curling shot with the outside of his foot. Once again the ball goes in the net, but only after a slight deflection by Andy's teammate, Charlie, who wasn't even looking. The goal goes to Charlie, and we're back to a new kickoff.

SHE. Well, actually you've got it wrong. I'm not an expert, but I imagine the rules must go something like this: If Andy's shot is actually directed squarely at the net, then the goal is credited to Andy even if the ball is accidentally deflected by a defender or by a teammate. On the other hand, if Andy's shot is heading somewhere else but ends up in the net as a result of a deflection, then the goal is classified as an own goal by Bill or as a regular goal by Charlie (as the case may be), regardless of the deflection being unintentional. Let's not worry about the first case, which might have to be specified further. The second case seems reasonable enough, though: if it were not for the deflection, the goal wouldn't have been scored. Therefore, although it was Andy who did all the important work, the goal cannot be credited to him because the ball would not have gone in absent Bill's or Charlie's intervention (accidental as that might have been).

HE. Just a minute. It is true that, without the deflection, the ball would not have gone into the net. But it's also true that the ball wouldn't have gone into the net without the kick. And the kick was Andy's.

SHE. Well, then, something must be wrong with our intuitions about responsibility and causation. Think about it. What does it mean to say that a person is responsible for an accident? It means that had she not done what she did, the accident would not have occurred. What do we mean when we say that a certain event caused another? That if the first event had not occurred, the second would not have occurred either. So far so good. But what happens when the link between an action (or event) and its consequences is not so straightforward? Had the ball not been deflected, there would have been no goal. But as you said, had the ball not been kicked in the first place, there wouldn't have been a goal either. So who is responsible for the goal?

HE. That's exactly the problem. But where do you stop, once you've started tracing the chain of responsibilities back through time? Because pretty soon you find that the goal has to be credited to Andy's grandfather.

SHE. Consider the following scenario. Andy blasts a shot that is headed straight into the net. But Bill and Charlie both move into the ball's way, one behind the other. Bill kicks it off its path, so no score. But even if Bill had not managed to deflect it, the shot would have accidentally bounced off Charlie. So what do we say in this case? Should Bill get credit for the save?

HE. Not quite. After all, the ball was not going to score anyway; it would have hit Charlie's body.

SHE. But neither would it be right to say that anything happened thanks to Charlie. After all, Charlie did nothing.

HE. But then who is responsible for spoiling Andy's shot?

SHE. Cases like this one are indicative of a deep conceptual tension. I am walking in the rain. My umbrella is open and I am wearing a hat, so my head is not getting wet. But why is that so? It's not because of the umbrella, because I'm wearing my hat. And it's not because of my hat, for I have an umbrella. Or: Andy throws a stone against a window and Bill catches it before the impact. The owners of the store would like to thank Bill, but Charlie was standing right behind him at the time, and it is obvious that in any case the stone would have hit him, not the window. So do they thank Charlie instead?

HE. I suppose the law must be full of cases of this sort.

SHE. Nonetheless, the problem is more of a theoretical one than a practical one. These are situations about which we just don't know what we can say.

HE. Why not just cut the Gordian knot? Let's thank both Bill and Charlie. Let's thank your hat and your umbrella, or rather, the pair consisting of your hat and the part of the umbrella directly above it.

SHE. I'm not sure it's a good suggestion. All Gordian solutions leave everybody unhappy.

HE. But at least we can rely on it to overcome the unfairness of the top-scorer lists. Let us classify a deflected goal as an *ex aequo*. If one's shot ends up in the net as a result of another's ricochet, let us say that both did their part. Each player gets half a goal, whether good or bad.

There may be something disturbing in combining quotidian puzzles about soccer with situations that seem much more far-fetched (duplicate worlds, time travel). Nonetheless, the characters in our stories find themselves dealing with the many facets of a common problem—the problem of Cause and Effect. The poor fellow who leaves a pile of bewildered messages on his friend's answering machine is not out of his mind when he wonders about his Freedom; what could help him decide whether his actions are caused by his own Will or by his doppelganger? Before fantasizing about what one would do if one could travel in time, one should ponder what one could do; what could our actions cause, if the before comes after and the after, before? He and She settle on an arbitrary way out of the many-causes puzzle, with a fifty-fifty solution that will leave many a Reader disappointed. But why the disappointment? Perhaps our concept of causation is just not made to fit such cases? The quandaries we have already run into will be silently lying in wait for us in much of what follows. Philosophy is often the offshoot of unexpected conceptual tensions—of difficulties that arise when we try to apply the concepts we are most familiar with to situations that are not familiar at all. We have to test the elasticity of our conceptual scheme, but in order to do that, we sometimes have to envisage fantastic scenarios in which our concepts are stretched to the limit. This will be clearer as we proceed to chapter

2

in which old and new characters discover that the Mind is an elusive entity, that they can talk in their sleep and leave their interlocutor wondering in bewilderment whether they are Conscious or not, that tastes are anything but easy to define, that without memories it may well be impossible to speak of Responsibility—and perhaps even of Persons—and in which the nosy Meddler will demonstrate that the Brain is even more elusive than the Mind, to the point that in a Brain transplant, it is almost better to be a donor than a receiver.

ZOMBIE, INC. SLEEPING PILLS

STEWARD'S VOICE. Fasten your seat belts.

HE, *courteously getting up from his seat.* Let me let you through. These seats can be very uncomfortable.

PASSENGER. Thank you. I'm not exactly a fan of economy class, either. (*Opens her purse.*) I'm going to take a pill right away.

HE. "Zombie" sleeping pills? Sounds strong. I gather our conversation ends here . . . Shall I wake you up before landing?

PASSENGER. Oh, don't worry. The pill will only blunt my consciousness; all my other intellectual and physical functions will be unaffected. I'll be able to speak with you, watch the movie, fill out the immigration papers. It's a good way to get through the flight without looking like a bag of potatoes.

HE. What do you mean? If you lose consciousness, don't you fall asleep?

PASSENGER. This is what happens from *my* point of view. The pill results in total blackout, and the light comes back when the effect is over. But from *your* point of view, nothing changes. I will continue to speak, to answer your questions—even to ask questions—and you won't be able tell the difference.

HE. I'm not sure I understand . . .

PASSENGER. There is a large philosophical literature on zombies—imaginary creatures that behave in every respect like normal human beings but lack consciousness altogether. Our company managed to get hold of the idea and invested millions to patent the Zombie sleeping pills. You see, consciousness is a very feeble phenomenon—a light froth on top of the oceanic depths of the mind. If you remove the froth, the waves do not change. The mind continues to function even without consciousness. After all, the brain is a machine for processing information; since my eyes are open, my brain keeps registering and processing all incoming information, and it keeps controlling my actions and decisions. The only difference is that nowhere in my mind is the consciousness-show taking place. But that show is just a luxury, an esthetic *caprice*—as I said, consciousness is just a spray of foam on the surface of a deep and unfathomable ocean.

HE. I actually read that only we human beings have the privilege of consciousness. According to Descartes, cats and dogs are mere automata—like zombies, if I understand correctly.

PASSENGER. Which does not prevent us from treating cats and dogs in a different manner than we treat robots. As a matter of fact, you're treating me in a perfectly normal way, too—you're not treating me as if I were a zombie.

HE. You're right. But how long before the sleeping pills take effect?

PASSENGER. Oh, they take immediate effect. As soon as I took the pill I lost consciousness. You can't tell, but I'm fast asleep.

HE. Good grief! Do you mean to say that you have been speaking in your dreams?

PASSENGER. Dreams? Not at all, otherwise there would be no zombie effect. My dream would be indistinguishable from reality, so why take the pills? Descartes himself said that dreaming is a form of consciousness. No, right now my mind must be totally blacked out.

HE. I'm not sure I want to continue this conversation. . . . But how can you tell whether you are awake or asleep?

PASSENGER. I know these pills are a good product, so I can safely say that at this moment I am completely unconscious. Here, have a look at the brochure. I have fallen into deep, dreamless cataplexy. But, as I said, this has no effect on my interactions with the world around me. Perhaps this conversation is bothering you? I'm very sorry if it is.

HE. No, on the contrary! Have you been with Zombie, Inc., for a long time, if I may ask?

PASSENGER. A couple of years—why?

HE. I was wondering how your product is doing on the market. I read somewhere that some people think consciousness is a curse in some ways, and not just because of the annoyance of flying. There are many circumstances in our lives when we would be a lot happier if we didn't know what was going on, so I wouldn't be surprised if you told me that you have plenty of customers.

PASSENGER. Oh, very many indeed. As I was boarding the aircraft, I noticed that even our pilots have a good supply of our product. I can only sympathize: it must be awfully boring to cross the ocean four times a month.

HE. What? This aircraft is being flown by zombies?

PASSENGER. Don't worry. The pills have been tested and certified by all international medical authorities. Actually, since you look a bit anxious, why don't you take a pill, too?

HE. Thank you. So this will soon be a conversation between two zombies. I guess I should take a few notes if I want to remember what happened.

PASSENGER. That's not necessary. The Zombie pills efface consciousness in the present, but all experience gets recorded somewhere, and we can always *remember* it later. When we wake up, we won't be two strangers but two people who shared a pleasant afternoon talking philosophy. Indeed, our whole personal identity is built on memory—the memory of the events that make up our life.

PARTIAL AMNESIA

FROM: K. J., PRISONER

TO: THE DIRECTOR OF THE PENITENTIARY

Dear Director, forgive me if I take the liberty of writing again to reiterate my query (see my letters of February 10 and February 21). Since when have I been held in custody at this penitentiary, and what are the reasons for my detention? I realize it may sound absurd but, as I have tried to explain, I don't seem to be able to recall either the crimes for which I have been convicted or the date of my imprisonment. Would you be so kind as to remind me?

FROM: MEDICAL OFFICER

TO: THE DIRECTOR OF THE PENITENTIARY

This is to certify that Mr. K. J., held in custody at the State Penitentiary for the Smith affair, has undergone serious memory loss as a result of a fall. Our analyses show that Mr. K. J. is suffering from irreversible amnesia regarding all the events in connection with the crime for which he is being detained, as well as for other facts related to the trial and the date of his imprisonment. As for the rest, all of his intellectual and emotional faculties appear to be intact.

"DAILY NEWS," FROM OUR LOCAL CORRESPONDENT

Officers at the State Penitentiary are facing an unusual deontological conundrum. Mr. K. J., found guilty in relation to the Smith affair, appears to have lost all memory of his crimes. During his period of incarceration, Mr. K. J. is reported to have given clear signs of remorse, repeatedly asking to be forgiven for whatever despicable acts he might have committed. A model prisoner, he is also the promoter of an initiative called "The Power of Remembrance," which aims to help all prisoners who have an opportunity to reenter society by getting them to focus on their memories of their misconduct. The administration of the penitentiary is considering the situation. At the moment, it has not even been decided whether Mr. K. J. should be informed of the reasons of his incarceration, for fear of further traumatic consequences.

FROM: M. SMITH

TO: THE DIRECTOR OF THE PENITENTIARY

Dear Director, I have been informed that Mr. K. J. is being kept ignorant of the reasons for his incarceration. I think we had better refresh his memory. This individual committed infamous acts that stained the good name of our family, and I don't see why we should be the only ones to carry the burden of this recollection. I hope no one will say that K. J. is a different person today from the one who was found guilty, just because he has now forgotten what he did. I have certainly forgotten many episodes of my past, but nobody would even dream of treating me as another person. That idea that personal identity depends on the memory of our past experiences is an interesting philosophical theory of the Empiricists, but here we are no longer in college.

FROM: L. SMITH

TO: THE DIRECTOR OF THE PENITENTIARY

Dear Director, I am writing in strong support of the move to pardon Mr. K. J., who pleaded guilty in relation to the scandal that hit my family two years ago. I understand that the medical appraisal has established beyond all doubt that Mr. K. J. has lost all memory of his crimes due to an irreversible form of partial amnesia. I therefore find it cruel and unfair to condemn him to serve a sentence for an event that has been completely deleted from his mind. From this point of view, Mr. K. J. is no different from any person who, without having committed any crime, wakes up one morning in jail faced with the prospect of serving a sentence for reasons that are utterly mysterious to him.

FROM: K. J., PRISONER

TO: THE DIRECTOR OF THE PENITENTIARY

Dear Director, despite your much-appreciated discretion, I have now come to learn of my own amnesiac disorder, as well as the reasons that led to my imprisonment in this penitentiary. I am therefore writing to express my firm intention of serving my full sentence. On the basis of the information that has been disclosed to me, there is no question that I am guilty as charged and consequently that I have to serve the total term or terms to which I have been sentenced, even though I continue to lack any memory of the crimes that I seem to have committed. I do not, in fact, believe that memory is the only criterion for deciding the identity of a person, nor that the subject should be the ultimate judge of his or her own knowledge. There are objective conditions for knowledge and responsibility that transcend the powers of the subject.

FROM: THE STATE LEGAL OFFICE

With reference to the plea for a pardon on behalf of prisoner K. J.: Insofar as it is justified by considerations of personal identity, it is reasonable to maintain that a sentence should generally not depend on the convict's psychological condition subsequent to the criminal act, but only on the conditions concomitant to the act (for example, an inability to understand the nature of what he or she was doing). It is nonetheless reasonable to maintain that the sentence itself loses its value if the convict is unable to connect it to some memory of the criminal act, given that under such circumstances the relevant conditions of personal identity are uncertain. In the absence of precise guidelines, this Office is not in a position to deliberate on the plea. We therefore recommend a thorough investigation of the criteria by which we determine the personal identity of those to whom the penal code applies.

PERSON TRANSPLANT

HE, *stopping in front of a glass door.* What a terrible headache. (*Reads the sign on the door and grows excited.*) "Zoom Clinic. Transplants. Any organ." *Any* organ? Exactly what I need. (*Enters.*) Good morning.

NURSE. Good morning. May I help you?

HE. You do organ transplants, right?

NURSE. Yes sir. It's our specialty.

HE. Of any organ, if I understand correctly.

NURSE. Absolutely. Without false modesty, we are among the very few centers in the world that can offer a complete service. Over two hundred organs: vital and auxiliary, internal and external . . . you name it. Here's the whole list.

HE. You also perform brain transplants? I would really like to replace mine—I get such terrible headaches.

NURSE. Of course. Just fill out this form. Date of birth and all that.

HE, *picking up the form and beginning to write.* Profession . . . address . . . and what should I write here?

NURSE. Where?

HE. Here. You want to know whether I wish to be a *donor* or a *receiver*.

NURSE. Yes, you have to choose. In the first case, you make your brain available to those who might be interested in it. In the second case, you place a request for a new brain, and we'll check to see what is available.

HE. Hmm, I don't know . . . Is there a price difference?

NURSE. As a donor, you must pay ten thousand dollars. As a receiver, we pay you ten thousand dollars.

HE. Wow! That's a big difference. I could certainly use ten grand! So I'll go for receiver.

NURSE. Very well. Please sign here . . .

THE MEDDLER, *coming in from a side door.* Wait!

NURSE. What? Who are you?

THE MEDDLER. I'm telling you, think about it.

HE. About what?

THE MEDDLER. About the fact that they pay you as a receiver but not as a donor. Since when do people pay to give something and get paid to receive something?

NURSE. Well, sometimes it happens. For instance, there's a tax on garbage: all citizens must pay to get rid of it, and the city is paid to collect it.

HE. Right. That's exactly why I want to be paid. If I were the one to pay, my brain would be like garbage.

THE MEDDLER. Don't say that again, because somebody might take you seriously. Anyway . . . (*The phone rings.*)

NURSE. Zoom Clinic, how can I help you? Yes . . . a brain transplant? As a donor? Very well . . . You have already paid the full amount? Of course . . . As a matter of fact, we have a receiver in the clinic right now. Shall I ask him? . . . All right then, thank you. Have a nice day. (*Hangs up.*)

HE. Did I hear correctly? I have a donor?

NURSE. Exactly. If you agree, we could do the whole thing tomorrow. You will leave here with a brand new brain and a check for ten thousand dollars.

THE MEDDLER. Come on, think about it. What does it mean to get a new brain?

HE. I suppose it's like getting a new liver. Or a new heart. Or a new left arm.

NURSE. Or a whole new body! We transplant absolutely everything!

THE MEDDLER. Right. But if they transplant everything, what remains of *you*?

HE. But I don't want to get everything transplanted. I just want a new brain.

THE MEDDLER. Put it this way. Suppose you had everything transplanted—everything except your brain. Wouldn't that be like transplanting your brain into a different body?

HE. I suppose so . . .

THE MEDDLER. So it would be like donating your brain. Thus, to go back to our case, your brain donor automatically becomes a receiver of your body. So you, the brain receiver, become a body donor.

HE. Eh? I don't want to sign up as a body donor. It would cost me a fortune!

NURSE. Nonsense. Just sign here and forget about it.

THE MEDDLER. Never mind the money! Your brain is not just an organ. Your brain is *you*. Don't get rid of it so easily.

HE. I am my brain? Perhaps this is what scientists and materialist philosophers maintain, but I might not agree. What is your line, here at the clinic?

NURSE. You could always have one half of your brain transplanted tomorrow, and the other half at a later time. Our clinic considers the two brain hemispheres as two distinct organs. Let me check . . . the file says that we pay five thousand dollars for each hemisphere, so the total would still be ten thousand.

HE. This is an excellent suggestion.

THE MEDDLER. Think about it, I said. There is only one way you could survive the first transplant, and that is if your personhood is completely contained in the original hemisphere you still have left. Otherwise, the person coming out of the operation wouldn't be *you*, but someone else. But then we're back to where we were: replacing one half of your brain is tantamount to donating the rest of your body!

NURSE. We have made partial transplants of both types: right hemisphere and left hemisphere. I can assure you that in both cases our patients have survived perfectly well.

THE MEDDLER. I doubt we agree on the meaning of "survive," but never mind. Suppose you are right. Then you must admit that independently of which hemisphere is transplanted first, after the operation, our patient will have donated the rest of his body.

HE. But then I would end up paying twice as a body donor while making the profit of a single brain receiver. Forget about it! (*Ponders.*) What if I got a transplant of both hemispheres at the same time, but from different donors? In that case, neither donor could claim to be the receiver of the rest of my body, so I wouldn't have to pay anything . . .

NURSE. And you would still earn your ten thousand as a brain receiver. Sounds perfect to me.

HE. Then it's a deal. Where do I sign?

THE MEDDLER. Deal? Listen to me. Your brain is not just an organ, no matter how you split it. It is you in person. Rather than replacing it, I suggest you start using it.

MY ICE CREAM, YOUR ICE CREAM

HE. How is your ice cream?

SHE. Good. Pistachio and strawberry. Yours?

HE. Strawberry and pistachio.

SHE. Same flavor, then.

HE. Almost. Yours is pistachio and strawberry, mine is strawberry and pistachio. Close your eyes and have a taste. Here is my strawberry.

SHE, *with her eyes closed*. But this is pistachio!

HE. I told you they're not the same!

SHE. Come on. You ask me to close my eyes and then you cheated. You said "strawberry," but it was pistachio.

HE. Not at all. Look, try the green one and tell me if it doesn't taste like strawberry.

SHE. Wait a moment—the green one is pistachio!

HE. That's what everybody says. To me the green one tastes like strawberry and the red one like pistachio. To you the red is strawberry and the green—pistachio. Right?

SHE. Perhaps they used different colorants for your ice cream?

HE. No. We bought it at the same place, remember?

SHE, *scrutinizing her ice cream*. You're not making fun of me? You are sincerely saying that the *green* flavor is strawberry to you and pistachio to me?

HE. And vice versa: the *red* flavor is strawberry to you and pistachio to me.

SHE. But isn't it just a matter of names? Perhaps when you were a child you were taught to call the "strawberry flavor" what I was taught to call the "pistachio flavor"—and vice versa.

HE. You really think badly of my parents, don't you? It doesn't stop with strawberry and pistachio either.

SHE. You mean to say . . .

HE. I mean to say that those yellow, juicy things that taste like lemons to you, taste like blueberries to me, and those small, blue things that taste like blueberries to you have the taste of lemon to me. That's why I like to put blueberries on my pistachio ice cream—so I have the impression of eating strawberries with lemon.

SHE, *very puzzled*. You must be wrong . . .

HE. Of course I am! I am wrong about all tastes.

SHE. No, that's not what I meant. There's something wrong with what you're telling me. You're saying that your parents didn't play tricks with you. They taught you to speak English like me, correct? So they would give you pistachio ice cream and they would say: "This tastes like pistachio."

HE. That's right.

SHE. And the ice cream had a certain flavor to you, correct? A flavor that you called "pistachio."

HE. Yes.

SHE. So why do you call it "strawberry" now?

HE. Because in the meantime everything has changed! As I was grow-
ing up, my sense of taste got switched around. At some point, strawberries
began to taste like pistachios and lemons like blueberries. All of a sudden.
Nothing serious, really: in a way I enjoyed it—and I still do. I often find
myself experimenting with new combinations.

SHE. But how can I be sure that you're not making this up? (*She notices
his mortified expression.*) Sorry, I didn't mean to offend you. I do trust you.
I was just playing the skeptic.

HE, *still bitter.* Don't mention it.

SHE. I always thought that when philosophers talked about these things,
they were just dealing with imaginary situations. I am surprised to learn
that it is not always like that . . . But wait—you still look sad!

HE. I was thinking that perhaps I really am mistaken. Perhaps I didn't
suffer a taste switch after all.

SHE. What do you mean?

HE. Perhaps I don't *remember* what things tasted like when I was small.
Perhaps this whole story is just a memory illusion: I didn't suffer a taste
switch but a memory switch. I *seem* to remember that strawberry ice cream
had a different flavor than it has now.

SHE. I can believe you when you say that your sense of taste got switched
around. I can overcome skepticism about other peoples' minds. But I can't
see how *you* can overcome skepticism about your own memories.

HE. Oh dear, and now my ice cream has melted, too.

SHE. So has mine . . . Well, now one *really* can't tell strawberry from
pistachio, or pistachio from strawberry—so at least that problem is gone.

HE. And we can be sure that our ice creams taste exactly the same.

So here's something to keep in mind: even if your travel companion does turn out to be completely deprived of an interior, subjective life, there is nothing to stop you from treating her as a person. If that is at odds with the Reader's views on Persons, we quite understand. It is precisely to stress the point that we decided to publish the correspondence of the amnesiac prisoner, in which the conceptual tension between having a past and knowing it gives rise to an authentic dilemma about the attribution of Responsibility—hence about the definition of Personhood. We do not, however, make any excuses for those who think that Persons have little to do with Brains, as the Zoom Clinic nurse seems to think; what the Meddler has to say about that strikes us as one hundred percent right. And we can only feel sorry for those who insist on the existence of internal, purely subjective criteria for verifying an individual's own intuitions about Subjectivity, unless a melted ice cream is a good enough consolation prize. All of which could also be regarded as a preamble to chapter

3

in which Chance makes its appearance and regularly spoils our characters' attempts to keep it under Control, distracted as they are by the elegant image they form of themselves—and of History, too.

PLAYING LOTTO IN REVERSE CITY

HE *gets off the bus and starts walking toward a grocery store. A* CITIZEN *comes out. She looks happy;* HE *addresses her in a jubilant voice.* Excuse me, madam, can you play Lotto here?

CITIZEN. Sure!

HE. Then I'm headed inside. I'm truly addicted: I just love trying my luck. I'm sure you understand . . .

CITIZEN. I play, too, but mostly out of necessity. Like now, for example. I had to buy some ice cream and I needed three dollars.

HE. Then you're a lucky player. I gather you've won more than three dollars—you must be pleased . . .

CITIZEN. Won? In what sense? I'm pleased I haven't lost anything!

HE. Haven't lost anything? What do you mean? How can you lose playing Lotto?

CITIZEN. All Lotto tickets here are black on white, but I notice that the one sticking out of your pocket is white on black. You're from Straight Town, aren't you, where people pay money to play Lotto, and occasionally win. But this is Reverse City, where people get paid to play Lotto, and occasionally lose.

HE. Fantastic! I was not aware of this way of trying one's luck. How does it work?

CITIZEN. Very simple. You just go to the NegaLotto and ask for a Scratch & Go ticket. Along with the ticket, you get one dollar. You scratch and see whether you have lost.

HE. And if I have lost?

CITIZEN. Then you pay, of course.

HE. How much?

CITIZEN. It depends on what it says on the ticket.

HE. But . . . if it says that I have lost a lot?

CITIZEN. If you've lost a lot you pay a lot—what else? I think the maximum one can pay is one million dollars.

HE. One million dollars? But that's crazy! Why should one risk bankruptcy just to get one dollar?

CITIZEN. I don't find it crazy at all. Here the game works that way.

THE MEDDLER, *from behind the cash register.* Indeed, may I remind you that the inclusion of an element of risk was the theme that inspired Borges's "The Lottery in Babylon," in which the citizens of that fantastic city put their existence under the aegis of Luck. It was a way to add flavor to their lives.

HE. Add flavor to their lives? It's appalling that someone might be willing to risk impoverishment in order to . . . buy some ice cream.

THE MEDDLER, *pompously.* One plays to win, but the excitement comes from the risks one takes. The real player is the one who can look at the prize she has won and pronounce Ulrich von Hutten's motto, "I dared!"

HE. Maybe. But to me it's plain folly—like Russian roulette.

CITIZEN. Well, here in Reverse City we see things the other way around (obviously). We think *your* game is plain folly.

HE. Why so, if I may ask?

CITIZEN. Here, there is a tiny chance that we may have a stroke of bad luck and lose money, sometimes even quite a lot of money, but with the vast majority of tickets, we don't lose a penny. On the contrary, we make a buck every time. You see? I needed three dollars for the ice cream and I asked for three tickets—and, as I expected, each ticket said "You've lost nothing!"

HE. Whereas in Straight Town . . .

CITIZEN. In Straight Town, there is a tiny chance that you may have a stroke of good luck and win money, maybe even quite a lot of money, but with the vast majority of tickets you don't make a penny. On the contrary, you lose a buck every time. Let me check your ticket . . . Just as I thought: "Try again, you may be lucky!" You see? Every day thousands of your people throw away a dollar just for the sake of trying their luck. I find that utterly absurd.

HE. But . . . but . . . sometimes someone wins! And that's why every-body plays Lotto in Straight Town. There is a great feeling of hope.

CITIZEN. Hope? I don't get it. You know perfectly well that you have an infinitely small chance of winning, and that it's almost certain that you'll lose a dollar. How can you be attracted by a game with a payoff like that?

HE. Hope never dies.

CITIZEN. Nonsense. You're just saying that to justify a behavior that is totally irrational. Compare your way with ours: we have an infinitely small chance of losing versus an almost certain probability of making a dollar. Now that's a good reason to play, don't you agree? Come on, let me buy you a coffee.

HE. Thanks, but I've already troubled you enough.

CITIZEN. No trouble at all. I just need to ask for two Scratch & Go tickets . . . Here they are. And as you see, we also got our two dollars. Now we scratch . . . and of course . . . we've lost nothing.

HE. I'm pleased!

CITIZEN. You see? At Reverse City we're all pleased.

HE. And as far as I know, the probability of losing twice in a row is very low. In case one really has a stroke of bad luck, one can always make up for it by asking for a whole bundle of tickets!

CITIZEN. Now we're beginning to understand each other. What's bet-ter: to give a dollar when you're almost certain you won't win, or to get a dollar when you're almost certain you won't lose? Believe me, the call is obvious.

LUCKY NUMBERS

HE. . . . at which point a bolt of lightning hit the car I was driving, I lost control, and I ended up in the middle of a rice field. Yet I walked away perfectly unharmed.

SHE. That was close!

HE. You can say that again. I should play Lotto! There must be a number for "struck by lightning."

SHE. Don't tell me you believe that we can read clues to our fate?

HE. Not really, but . . .

TRAVELING SALESMAN, *butting in boldly*. And why not? Today playing Lotto is a science. It's no longer a matter of superstition.

HE AND SHE. I beg your pardon?

SALESMAN. Let me put it this way. Lotto is a matter of statistics. Every number has the same probability of being drawn as any other, true enough. But we also know very well that a number cannot wait too long before coming up; the longer you wait for it, the higher the probability that it will come up. Our firm has developed a computer program that allows our customers to keep track of the frequency of appearance of each number in every known lottery, and it's selling like hot cakes. Mathematics, not superstition! Here, take it, this is our demo. It comes with the complete database. You can update it after every drawing, over the Internet. Keep an eye on number 27 in the next . . .

SHE. That's very generous of you, thanks. But I am afraid you're contradicting yourself. If every number has the same probability as any other number in any draw, why should a certain number be more likely to come up than the others in a specific draw?

SALESMAN. Because its turn is long overdue! We have been waiting for the 27 for a long time and it hasn't come up yet, so it must come up soon!

SHE. And why should this delay have any effect on the next draw, if I may ask? The next draw is completely independent of the previous ones. It cannot "see" into the past. Unless it's biased . . .

SALESMAN. No bias—it's purely a matter of statistics. It is just very unlikely that the number 27 should not come up after such a long delay. If you agree that the number 27 is in the same boat as any other number, then you must agree that it must come up, too, like the others.

SHE. It depends on how you measure your so-called delays.

SALESMAN. What do you mean? I just measure it by looking at the series of the previous draws.

SHE. The problem is how you identify this series. If you take a slightly different sequence, for instance, the series consisting of every second draw, then the frequencies might be very different. Indeed, we can check that directly on my laptop using your program . . . Just a moment . . . See? If we look at this other series, we should expect the number 59, not 27. And if we take the series consisting of every third draw . . . we should expect the number 6! And if . . .

SALESMAN. Hold on! Why on earth should we look at series like those? We must look at the sequence of *all* previous draws.

SHE. Well, there simply is *no reason* to prefer that series to the others. Every draw is independent of the previous ones, you agree on that. Lotto is blind; it can't see into the past. So every series is just as informative. The earlier draws do not really count.

SALESMAN. They don't count? You mean to tell me that if we toss a coin and we get heads three times in a row, I shouldn't bet on tails?

SHE. I do indeed. You are free to bet as you like, but the probability that the coin comes up tails is sure to be exactly fifty percent. If the coin is fair, then the tosses are independent events, so a run of heads cannot *increase* the probability of tails on a succeeding toss, no matter how long the run of heads is. At best, it may provide evidence that the coin or the method by which it is tossed is not fair. In that case, however, I would advise you to bet on heads again, not on tails!

SALESMAN. But tails is terribly late. Look at the series . . .

SHE. If you really wish to take the series into account, think of it this way: the probability of the series head-head-head-head is exactly the same as that of the series head-head-head-tail.

HE. Still, if you're right, then the fact that I was struck by lightning would in no way reduce my chances of being struck again. But I am sure that very few people are struck by lightning *twice*. I have already gone through it, so now I feel rather safe . . .

SALESMAN. Exactly!

SHE. Sorry to disappoint you, but I would recommend that you install a lightning rod. Perhaps you feel better off than me with regard to the next thunderstorm. But if I had to bet on which of us is more likely to be struck twice, I would bet on you.

HE. On me?

SHE. Of course. You've already been struck once, so you only need one more strike to get to two, whereas my count (and this gentleman's too, I daresay) is still at zero!

HE. So what *would* be the best way to win the Lotto, if I may ask?

SALESMAN. Right. What is your answer?

SHE. There's no best way to win, but there's a perfectly foolproof way not to lose. Just don't play!

THE INVISIBLE DISORDER

SHE. Let's say 1 is heads and 0 is tails. Suppose we toss a coin four times in a row. We could get the outcome 1111, that is, head-head-head-head.

HE. We could, but it would be very strange. It would be too *regular* as an outcome. So it's unlikely that we would get it.

SHE. I don't see any difference with respect to 0000, tail-tail-tail-tail.

HE. Indeed. The two sequences are equally improbable.

SHE. Then take 0011.

HE. This is also too regular, hence improbable (as is 1100). The 0s are grouped on one side, the 1s on the other.

SHE. What about 0110?

HE. Again, too much order (as with the twin series 1001). There is a perfect *symmetry* between 1s and 0s.

SHE. Let's see: 1010?

HE. Equally improbable. It's a perfect *alternation* of 1s and 0s (as is 0101, of course).

SHE. What can I suggest—perhaps 1000?

HE. We're wasting our time. As with 0111, 1110, and 0001, this configuration is too simple and ordered, don't you agree? What we get as a rule is: one-outcome-together-with-three-repetitions-of-the-other.

SHE. Would you say the same thing about the group 1011, 1101, 0100, 0010?

HE. Most definitely: the-singly-occurring-outcome-does-not-occur-at-the-beginning-or-at-the-end-of-the-sequence.

SHE. You started out by saying that a sequence such as 1111 is improbable because it is too regular. Now you are telling me that the other sequences that I have suggested are also too well organized. They all seem to follow a rule and none seems to be the product of chance. So you must say that they are all improbable. But then you are in trouble.

HE. Why?

SHE. The sequences that I have mentioned exhaust the range of *all* possible outcomes of four successive tosses of a coin. There are no other possibilities.

HE. In other words, if I toss a coin four times in a row, I am bound to get one of these sixteen sequences?

SHE. Yes. And that's the trouble. If the coin is fair, the outcome of your tosses must be dictated by chance. All the sequences that we have considered must therefore be dictated by chance. But according to you, they are all governed by some sort of order. And order rules out chance.

HE. Nobody would argue with me on the existence of order. Just look at the rules that govern the sequences: identities, symmetries, repetitions . . .

SHE. But if the sequence is truly the product of *chance*, how can it be *rule*-governed? No, my dear, the rules you are talking about are an illusion. They lie entirely in our minds, not in the reality of the sequences. The "rules" testify to our ability to "discover" some structure whenever we are confronted with a series of events. We are constantly on the alert, always looking for symmetries, configurations, repetitions, patterns. And we can always find them, if we wish.

HE. All right, let us suppose that the order is only imposed from the outside, a posteriori. I might agree that all the sequences we have considered are equally ordered, hence they would all have the same probability. But the objection is only valid for sequences consisting of four tosses. If you asked me to judge a sequence of six tosses, I would have to say that 010110, for example, is less ordered than 000000, or even than 000111.

SHE. I'm surprised. I had the impression that you were thinking along Wittgensteinian lines: give me a sequence whatsoever and I can find a rule of some sort that the sequence obeys (an outlandish rule, perhaps, but a rule nonetheless). I do, of course, agree that the feeling of "disorder" may increase as the sequence lengthens. Psychologists have performed a number of experiments that confirm this: we tend to regard 010110 as more probable than 000111, and the reason seems to be that 010110 looks more similar to a prototypical disordered sequence. Yet again this is an illusion: 010110 is just as probable as 000111.

HE. Then why is it we are so obsessed by the need to impose some order a posteriori?

SHE. It's our way to simplify the data. It is a useful simplification—it allows us to keep the enormous flow of information that hits us from all sides under control. Yet we must be aware of how things work. This order-seeking mechanism is always at work, even when there is no genuine order to be found. Think of Nostradamus's prophecies. They work well, right? *Too well*, with the wisdom of hindsight! It is obvious that someone filters the so-called prophecies in such a way as to make things work. Think of the obsessive (and perfectly useless, as we have already seen) hunt for a "delay" in a Lotto draw. Think of how we rewrite our lives by highlighting those facts that confirm the beautiful picture we have of ourselves, while disregarding those facts that don't bring us any credit. Think of the idea that history repeats itself—one of history's most repeated ideas. In all of these cases, we impose order on facts that we have every reason to regard as being overwhelmingly dominated by chance. We *enforce* order. But believe me: reality, life, and history are infinitely more complex than the images that we think we can make out in their texture.

That in our alphabetized and numericized world there are people who carry on playing Lotto or keep scanning the Past trying to figure out the Future shows that this world of ours is not so alphabetized and numericized after all. Hence we fear that empty questions about the Meaning of Life will continue to be taken for philosophical questions par excellence, and that whole forests will be cut down to produce tons of books discussing them. Such questions make as much sense as asking what the number of the world is, when everybody knows that the answer is 87, and in some cases, 23. But let's move on to chapter

4

which brings out the acumen of a solitary bell-ringer at the margins of the Empire, and in which an astonishing series of exotic journeys will show that Space and Time are tightly intertwined, and in which we will learn that lions have a remarkable sense of the Relativity of things, and will be led to wonder why mirrors reverse Left and Right but not Up and Down.

A MISSIVE FROM THE BELL-RINGER

FROM: BELL-RINGER NO. 2353, LAST VALLEY PARISH
TO: THE AUTHORITIES ON TIME, IN THE CAPITAL

BROTHERS,

I hope you will not regard this letter as inappropriate. I realize I am the last bell-ringer in the last parish of the Empire, the humblest, the most remote. But it is precisely for this reason that I feel obliged to write.

I have just read the Pamphlet issued by Your most excellent Authorities, entitled "On a New Method to Broadcast the Time Signal in the Empire," which I received by express stagecoach on May 20. Although I greatly appreciate the rigor of the Pamphlet and its insistence on the necessity of clear and unequivocal rules—so very important in this age of darkness and uncertainty—my impression is that the method, easy to apply as it may be, runs the risk of augmenting rather than diminishing the cloud of doubt. The pamphlet states that, as of today, the only Authority in command of the time signal is the Observatory in the Capital, which will ring its tower bell every hour. It is furthermore stated that the signal will have to be received and retransmitted by the bells on the outer circle of walls, and then by those in the suburbs, and so on and so forth from one parish to the next, from one town to another, spreading like the circles formed by a stone thrown into still water, until the last towers of the Empire are reached and the exact time—the sign of civilization—will come to the residents of the most remote valleys, like ours, which few wanderers visit. In conclusion, all bell-ringers are instructed to wait until they have distinctly heard each and every stroke before taking their turn and ringing their own bells, so as to be absolutely certain of the time to be signaled.

My misgivings, brothers, concern the consequences that this new method could have for the quality of the time signal. I venture to assert—in the hope that the hypothesis is not heretical—that time and space are much more closely intertwined than the honorable author of the Pamphlet has deemed. Consider what will happen. The signal originates in the Capital: the bell at the Observatory tolls six o'clock. The bell ringer of one of the towers on the outer wall hears the signal, waits until the sixth stroke, and then begins to ring his bells. And so on. The striking of six o'clock propagates slowly, because each bell ringer has to wait for the sound of the sixth incoming stroke before taking his turn. But, I repeat, space is time, and Last Valley lies 1,200 such turns or laps away from the Capital. A simple calculation will show that when the six bell strokes do reach our valley, it will be almost seven o'clock. Are people here supposed to live in permanent error?

Let me add a remark to indicate the paradoxical nature of the procedure. At midnight, the bell will toll twelve times. At one o'clock it will toll just once. Thus, the midnight signal will propagate slowly, much more slowly than the one o'clock signal, since in the first case the bell ringers will have to wait twelve full strokes before broadcasting the signal in their turn, whereas in the second case they will only have to wait a moment. I have done my calculations, and it turns out that I will have to strike one o'clock before midnight. Not only does space mean time; in this case, space appears to produce a contraction of time. Will the people of Last Valley have to live by time that coils around itself and then unwinds again every night, with hours that get longer and longer, balanced by hours of negative duration?

Thanking You for Your attention to the thoughts of this humble bell-ringer, etc.

PS: Should a position be available in a less secluded parish, would You be so kind to take my name into consideration? Here in Last Valley, life is pretty harsh, and I have now spent many decades amid these mountains.

FROM: THE AUTHORITIES ON TIME, IN THE CAPITAL

TO: BELL-RINGER NO. 2353, LAST VALLEY PARISH

BROTHER,

We have carefully examined your letter of June 21. Your concerns are legitimate, but they betray a misunderstanding of the principles that inspire these Authorities and as such they have been deemed heretical. In particular, it is the duty of these Authorities to determine a time that is valid in every parish of the Empire; this time, and its measurement, flow directly from the actions of the Authorities and are defined by such actions. Consequently:

First, your claim that the six o'clock strokes will reach your valley at seven is rejected. Time is measured by the bell tower at the Observatory; there is no simultaneity beyond that which is defined by its strokes and by their transmission. Hence when your bell does strike six o'clock, then and only then will it be six o'clock in Last Valley. Your "calculations" are refuted in so far as they place personal ambition above the orders of the Authorities.

Second, your reasoning concerning the putative "paradox" of the one o'clock signal, which will overtake the midnight signal, contains a severe fallacy.

In view of your age and of the well-known difficulties involved in a protracted stay in Last Valley, of which we are fully aware, these Authorities would be willing to grant you a less remote post, even to offer you a vacant position in the Capital. But first it is absolutely necessary that you recognize the faulty reasoning contained in your claim that because of the method envisaged by the Authorities you would have to strike one o'clock before midnight.

SPARKLING BUBBLES

STEWARD'S VOICE. Fasten your seat belts.

PASSENGER. Good evening. Sorry to bother you, but that's my seat. I always choose a window seat—to see the clouds from above.

SHE, *courteously getting up.* Yes, of course. At dawn it can be truly spectacular. I travel often, though, so I've seen it many times. Now I prefer the convenience of an aisle seat—to get up as often as I like without disturbing the person next to me. Besides, I must admit that tonight I would rather not travel at all.

PASSENGER. Why not? Flying on New Year's Eve is pretty original. And convenient, too: the fares are cheap and the airports aren't crowded.

SHE. Provided you make it there . . . With the traffic converging on Times Square, it took me more than an hour to get out of Manhattan. In any event, I don't find the idea of celebrating New Year's Eve in an airplane particularly exciting. I would have much preferred to avoid it.

PASSENGER. Not me; I find the idea thrilling! Apart from the convenience, it seems to me that a toast up in the sky is a truly unique opportunity. I even brought a bottle of champagne, in case the flight attendants don't have anything planned. See? It might not be ice cold, but I hope you won't stand on ceremony.

SHE. Very kind of you—thanks.

PASSENGER. More than anything else, I am thrilled by the idea of toasting several times in a row. You know, with all the time zones that we are going to cross I wouldn't be surprised if we got drunk . . .

SHE. Excuse me, but then you are on the wrong flight. If you want to toast repeatedly you must fly westward. Then you can celebrate at the stroke of midnight, and a few minutes later you enter a time zone where it is only 11 p.m.; you wait for midnight again and you can celebrate a second time, and so on and so forth. I understand that for the new millennium, the Paris–New York flights were anything but cheap. But here we are flying in the opposite direction; we are going eastward. We are leaving New York at 6 p.m., and a few minutes later it will already be 7 p.m., then 8 p.m. . . . and so on until 8 a.m., when we arrive in Paris, assuming the flight isn't delayed. No repeated toasts for us, I'm afraid. On the contrary, we must be quick if we don't want to find ourselves in the 1 a.m. time zone with the glass still full of champagne!

PASSENGER. Gosh, you're right! I always get confused when it comes to time zones and all that. I never know which direction saves you time. So at the time of our departure it will already be midnight in Europe . . .

Oh well, it's still going to be something special, don't you agree? If I understand you right, we are going to enter the 11 p.m. time zone in the middle of the ocean. So we will no longer be in the United States and not yet in Europe. This means that we are going to celebrate the stroke of midnight . . . in no-man's land! To me, that's more than enough for a very special toast.

SHE. If you say so . . . As far as I am concerned, I have always made a boast of the fact that I celebrate every new year either in Paris or in New York, and the idea of a toast in the middle of the ocean doesn't particularly attract me.

THE MEDDLER, *suddenly popping up from the seat in front*. Provided we are given a chance to make a toast.

PASSENGER. I beg your pardon?

THE MEDDLER. How can you be so sure that we are going to celebrate the stroke of midnight in the middle of the ocean?

PASSENGER. Well, if all goes according to schedule, it's just a mathematical fact. As this lady was saying, if we leave at 6 p.m. and arrive at 8 a.m., sooner or later we're going to hit midnight somewhere. And if my geography doesn't fail me, at that point, we are still going to be quite far from the coast of Europe.

THE MEDDLER. I'm sorry, but who told you that we are going to be somewhere *at midnight*? Have you studied the route so well?

PASSENGER. The route?

THE MEDDLER. Mathematics and geography tell us that during the flight it will happen more than once that we reach the stroke of the hour without leaving the time zone we are in. If our flight lasts eight hours and the time difference between New York and Paris is six hours, this will happen at least twice, and at most eight times. But there is no guarantee that the stroke of midnight will be among these cases. In fact, I did some calculations, and all things being equal, it turns out that we are going to skip midnight altogether. (This *does* deserve a special toast!)

PASSENGER. I'm still not following you.

SHE. Sounds pretty clear to me. Suppose that at 11:45 (local time), just as you are getting ready for the toast, we enter the next time zone. Then we automatically find ourselves at 12:45 (new local time) and fifteen minutes later it's already 1 a.m. You will find yourself with the bottle in your hands and the glasses still empty, and that's it. No midnight to celebrate.

PASSENGER. But then . . .

THE MEDDLER. But then nothing. Believe me, it will happen exactly like that. No midnight. No countdown. On this plane we are going to go from one year to the next without crossing the boundary.

PASSENGER. Darn! And I was even thinking that we were on our way to repeated celebrations. I am truly disappointed.

THE MEDDLER. Disappointed? I do it every year and, trust me, it's worth it. I am against all boundaries, even temporal ones. Toasting their absence is truly rewarding.

SHE. You guys are so bizarre . . . But I must admit, I hadn't thought about it. If things are really the way you say, then I have nothing to complain about anymore. I can still claim that I always celebrate New Year's Eve either in Paris or in New York. This trip won't be an exception.

PASSENGER. It won't be an exception because you won't be able to celebrate anything at all.

THE OTHERS. No, no, we *are* going to celebrate. But we are going to celebrate the absence of the magical moment. We shall give an early farewell to the old year and a late welcome to the new year. But we won't miss a single instant!

DATES OF BIRTH

BOY. Good morning, sir. I am here for the dinosaur exhibit. I understand that children under three don't have to pay . . .

BOX-OFFICE ATTENDANT. Correct. It is our latest initiative to promote the museum among our little friends.

BOY. Excellent! My parents told me about it just in time: I'm turning three tomorrow! Here is my ID.

ATTENDANT. Thank you. But . . . sorry . . . here it says that you were born on January 16. And that's today's date.

BOY. Sure, I know that. But a birth date says nothing by itself; you also have to check the place of birth. See, it's written right here: I was born on January 16, 2002, *in Los Angeles*. And please believe me if I tell you that I was born at 10:30 p.m. If you wish, I can bring a copy of my birth certificate.

ATTENDANT. I don't get it.

BOY. If I was born at 10:30 p.m. on January 16 in the city of Los Angeles, then at the time of my birth here in New York, it was already January 17. You know better than me that there is a three-hour time difference between the east and west coasts. So my birthday is on January 16 for the people in Los Angeles, but in New York, it's on January 17. Don't you agree?

ATTENDANT. I'm sorry, but here it says that you were born on January 16, and January 16 is today. You have *just* turned three, but you have *already* turned three. I am afraid there is nothing I can do.

GIRL, *waiting in line behind the boy, following the exchange with interest.* May I say something? It so happens that I too was born on January 17. See? This is my ID.

ATTENDANT. January 17, 2002. Very well. You can go in for free—just in time!

GIRL. Still, allow me to point out my place of birth: New York. Now, it so happens that I was born at 1:30 a.m. . . .

BOY. But then, Miss, you and I were born at exactly the same time!

GIRL. Indeed. We were born at the same time, but in two different time zones. (*Addressing the attendant.*) Thus, if you are willing to let me in for free, I don't see why you should not let him in for free, too. He is *exactly* my age.

ATTENDANT. There's nothing I can do about it. I must enclose a copy of your IDs, and these say that you were born on different dates: you on the 17th, he on the 16th.

GIRL. But sir, our IDs say more than that. They also say that I was born in New York and he was born in Los Angeles. Why don't we also add the information about the time of birth? Then the data would be complete: "Born in New York on January 17, 2002, 1:30 a.m." and "Born in Los Angeles on January 16, 2002, 10:30 p.m." These two pieces of information, different as they might appear, identify exactly the same instant of time.

ATTENDANT. Let me get this straight. I was born at 11 p.m. on February 29, in Boston. Are you saying that according to my uncles, who live in Rome, I was born on the 1st of March?

BOY AND GIRL. Indeed!

ATTENDANT. But on regular (nonleap) years, in the absence of February 29, I celebrate my birthday on March 1. Are you saying that if I moved to Italy, I would have to celebrate on March 2?

BOY AND GIRL. Yes, March 2.

ATTENDANT. But don't you find it strange that I should celebrate my birthday on the second day of March if I was born in February?

BOY AND GIRL. Strange, sir, but perfectly logical.

ATTENDANT. If you say so . . . Here, take your free tickets. I just hope I don't have to repeat the whole story to my superiors.

BOY. Thanks.

GIRL. And now, let's go to the pastry shop to celebrate our birthday!

ATTENDANT. Wait a minute. Haven't we gone through this whole complicated reasoning process precisely to establish that your birthday is tomorrow?

BOY AND GIRL. Yes, of course, our birthday is tomorrow. But we always celebrate one day in advance!

FOUR-SEASONS ISLAND

HE. Good morning. I'd like to make a reservation for the holidays. I was thinking of going somewhere in the Pacific.

TRAVEL AGENT. An excellent idea. Allow me to suggest Four-Seasons, the new artificial island.

HE. An artificial island?

AGENT. Yes, but don't worry. It looks and feels perfectly natural. Very wild and intimate, with plenty of vegetation and just four houses, not one more.

HE. That's interesting. I don't like crowded places. And where would this island be?

AGENT. On the equator, just where it meets the international date line.

HE. At the intersection of space and time! I have always been fascinated by this business of the international date line. How does it work, exactly?

AGENT. It's simple. Suppose that on the west side of the international date line it is midnight. On the other side, toward the east, it is already 1 a.m.; a new day has started. This new day—say, January 1—begins many times as we proceed westward; it goes around the world changing December 31 into January 1, until we get back around to the international date line. This means that midnight goes around the world changing one day into the next, but this change is not complete until we are back at the international date line. Until then, there will be lands that lie in December 31 and are still waiting to be hit by the new day, and lands that already lie in January 1.

HE. And when the midnight line has completed its tour around the world . . .

AGENT. At that point, it will be January 1 on the whole planet, and a second later, the midnight line will move westward, inaugurating January 2.

HE. So if the international date line passes through an inhabited zone, then someone could go from one day to another just by walking through it. You could go back to December 31 just by stepping eastward, and then decide to return to January 1 just by stepping westward!

AGENT. Right. And by doing so, you could also move from one year to the next—and back.

HE. Very amusing. I wouldn't mind spending my vacation on this island—what did you say it's called?

AGENT. Four-Seasons Island. For what date would you like your reservation?

HE. I would like to leave on June 21.

AGENT. All right. And when would you like to get there? Spring, summer, fall, or winter?

HE. I beg your pardon? I said I wanted to go on June 21.

AGENT. Yes, but when do you want to get *there*—spring, summer, fall, or winter?

HE. I guess I'm missing something. How long would the trip take?

AGENT. Oh, it's not the trip. It depends on the house you choose. If you stay in the northwestern house, then it will be summer. That house is north of the equator. But if you stay in the southwestern house, then it will be winter, since the two hemispheres have opposite seasons.

HE. I completely forgot about that! Well, I have to choose between summer and winter, right? Then I'll choose . . .

AGENT. Hold on, sir, I must interrupt you. You have two more options. You said you wanted to go on June 21. If instead of the southwestern house (winter) you choose the southeastern house, then you cross the international date line and you'll find yourself on June 20. And in the southern hemisphere, it's still fall on June 20.

HE. Don't tell me I can also go there in spring . . .

AGENT. Of course. All you have to do is cross the equator and go to the northeastern house: if it is fall in the southern hemisphere, then in the northern hemisphere, it will be spring.

HE. That's why you asked me *when* I want to get there! At the solstice, the "when" determines the "where." It's a tough choice . . .

AGENT. For a small surcharge I can give you all four houses.

HE. That's a great idea. Then I could walk around all the time, going from one season to another. It would be like living a thousand years. A holiday for the *Guinness Book of Records*!

AGENT. You could do better than that. When you get there, you can sit at the point of intersection between the equator and the international date line. If you stay there, you can be in all four seasons at the same time. Or outside the four seasons. Whichever you like!

LOST BEAUTY SPOTS

SHE. Good morning. I came to pick up my tickets for the Adventure Journey to the North Pole.

TRAVEL AGENT. Hem . . . (*Embarrassed.*) I think . . .

SHE. What's the matter? I thought it was all set. I paid a fortune for this trip—snowshoes, dog sled, masks, ice-breaker, a six-week survival course. Don't tell me . . .

AGENT. Unfortunately we've had to cancel the journey.

SHE. Cancel the journey? But why? The season is perfect, the weather forecast couldn't be better, nobody is on strike. Why did you cancel the journey?

AGENT. You're right, the conditions are as good as they could ever be. And believe me if I tell you that we worked very hard on this package. We are terribly sorry to disappoint our customers—but we just cannot take you to the North Pole.

SHE. What happened? You are speaking as though there were sudden, insurmountable difficulties.

AGENT. I don't know what to say. (*Pulls out a crumpled press clipping.*) Here, see for yourself.

SHE, *reading.* "The North Pole used to be here."

AGENT. Look at the picture. That's where the North Pole used to be. Now there's just water. It's the greenhouse effect—the ice is melting everywhere.

SHE. Oh, come on, I know the story. It was in every newspaper, but it's a hoax. We know perfectly well that the North Pole is not melting—not yet, at least. And even if it did? We could still go there by boat . . .

AGENT. Really? That's reassuring. Given the problem, we were thinking of organizing special trips to pay a tribute to the memory of all the lost beauty spots. We could take our customers to what used to be famous locations, locations that were famous due to something that's gone forever. Can you imagine the slogans on the brochures? "The Bamiyan Buddha statues used to be here, but now there's nothing but a pile of rubble"; "Lake Aral used to be here, but now it's a dried-up salt flat"; and so on. We could add: "The North Pole used to be here, but now it's just a place in the middle of the ocean."

SHE. Interesting. I'm sure you could put together a good list of locations, and find the customers, too. But . . .

AGENT. But what?

SHE. How do you interpret your slogans? To me they seem to have different meanings in each case.

AGENT. To me they all have the same meaning. Each slogan says that here—that is, in a certain place that is different in each case—there was something that is gone forever. Don't you agree? It's like saying, "My wallet was here." What else could I mean? My wallet was located here, and now it's gone. (*To herself.*) By the way, where *did* it go?

SHE. I disagree. The interpretation you are suggesting is all right for the Buddha statues. There is a certain place (Bamiyan), there was a certain object that was located there (a statue, or a bunch of them), and now the object no longer exists or is no longer in that place.

AGENT. Precisely.

SHE. But that's not quite the right thing to say in the Lake Aral case. Do you think a lake is just a mass of water?

AGENT. I wouldn't think so. There are many dry lakes. I would rather say that a lake is a place. When people say that Lake Aral has dried up, they mean to say that a certain place was full of water, and now the water is gone.

SHE. But then your slogan "Lake Aral used to be here" makes no sense. If Lake Aral were a place, how could it be right to say that it *was* but no longer *is* "here"? Places don't move.

AGENT. I see. Then, yes, I would say that a lake is a mass of water.

SHE. In which case, you are going to be in trouble when it comes to dry lakes, which are anything but masses of water. Not only that—if a lake is a certain mass of water, and the water gets channeled and diverted to the ocean, would you say that the lake has moved into the ocean? And what if we filled up the lake with new water? What if we filled it up with wine?

AGENT. Gosh . . . Perhaps our concept of a lake is a hybrid concept? We tend to think of a lake as a mass of water (or of some liquid stuff) but also as a place that can host a mass of water. Depending on the context, we go one way or the other.

SHE. Let's go back to the North Pole. What sort of thing is it? And what does it mean to say that it is no longer "here"?

AGENT. Right. Where did it go?

SHE. It didn't go *any*where. When we speak of the North Pole, we are using a purely spatial concept. There is no object corresponding to the North Pole. It's not like the Buddha statues, and it's not like Lake Aral, either. The North Pole can be made of anything. Or better, it is not made of anything. It is a pure receptacle, as Aristotle would say.

AGENT. Are you saying that the North Pole is an abstraction?

SHE. Not all things made of nothing are abstractions. If you dug a hole through the ice at the North Pole, you wouldn't be digging an abstraction. You would be digging a concrete hole, if I may say so.

AGENT. And where would the North Pole be, then?

SHE. Inside the hole. If we could remove the core of our planet as we remove the core of an apple, the terrestrial axis would extend through an empty region. But it would be there. The poles would be purely virtual.

AGENT. All right. But then such virtual places would not be part of our planet, would they?

SHE. I'm not sure what to say . . . anyway, you see now that the slogan "The North Pole used to be here" doesn't work? You must agree—the North Pole is still there.

AGENT. But why does the slogan sound so natural? Nobody found anything wrong with the phrase. As far as I know, the newspapers didn't get flooded with letters of complaint.

SHE. Purely spatial concepts tend to *adhere* to material objects. We can't think of a hole without thinking of a perforated object. And the best way to think of the North Pole is to think of the ice that is located at the North Pole. This picture of the North Pole as a huge piece of ice is deeply entrenched in our mind, and that is the picture we see when we read the headlines or sign up for an organized journey to the North Pole. We want to go and visit the glacial landscape that we mentally associate with the North Pole. If these are really the expectations of your customers, and if it were really true that the ice had melted, then canceling the journey is probably the right thing to do. But not because the destination has ceased to exist—it has changed, but it still exists. And if you intend to organize your new holiday packages—the guided visits to the lost beauty spots of the planet—you must make that distinction. In some cases, the slogan will say "The Bamiyan Buddha statues used to be here," and perhaps also "Lake Aral used to be here." But in other cases you must change the formula. You must say "The North Pole used to be *like this*."

HIC SUNT LEONES

LEA. Let's go and see the visitors.

LEO. Yeah, let's go. That's the one thing I like about living here at the zoo.

LEA. Every day we have new people to watch, and they all look so funny in their clothes, with their cameras, their sunglasses, their ice creams . . .

LEO. Feels like a madhouse.

LEA. I gather we have seen millions in the ten years we have been here. Good thing they managed to fence so many of them into this cage.

LEO. To *fence* them? In what sense?

LEA. Well, isn't there a guy who comes every day with a key, opens the gate, brings us food (a kind gesture, all the more so because there isn't much else to eat here), and then locks himself up with all the others?

LEO. Locks himself up—where?

LEA. Well, in the cage—where else?

LEO. Wait wait wait. I thought *we* were locked up in a cage. The guy brings us food—thank goodness—and then goes back to his free world. What makes you think that *they* are locked up, not *we*?

LEA. Maybe it's just a question of terminology. I take it that to be locked up means to be *inside* the cage. It means to be *behind* the bars. Perhaps to you it means something different?

LEO. No, it means exactly the same thing. It means to be inside the cage, behind the bars. That's why I'm saying that we are locked up.

LEA. But from our point of view, it is they who are standing behind bars.

LEO. Sure. From their point of view, however, we are the ones standing behind bars!

LEA. And why on earth should we adopt *their* point of view? Are we lions or are we not? We have our dignity!

LEO. Perhaps we disagree about the word "inside." To me, you are stuck inside the cage if you can't go out. Or maybe we disagree on the meaning of "cage."

LEA. Let's see. A cage is a wide space that surrounds the world. The world is a small, intimate place where you and I live happily. The cage has bars that separate it from the world and protects the population of the world (you and I) from the population of the prisoners (they), who can be very aggressive and dangerous. I don't see the problem. Let me say it again—are you a lion or what?

LEO. Yes I am, but evidently you don't see the problem. A cage is a small space and the world surrounds it. The world is a huge space where you and I could roam freely and happily. The cage has bars that separate it from the world and protects the world's population (they) from the prisoners (you and I), who can be very aggressive and dangerous. When was the last time we managed to eat a visitor?

LEA. So we disagree on the meaning of the word "cage." You seem to be thinking that a cage must be smaller than the rest of the world.

LEO. Indeed. I am pretty sure the dictionary that we found in the bag of the lion tamer we gobbled up a while ago will confirm that.

LEA. I don't trust dictionaries, especially if they come from the bag of some thick-headed lion tamer. But let's see . . . At the end of the dictionary they usually put a map of the world . . . Here it is. And look: *Hic sunt leones*. As you can see, there's a wide area south of the equator where it's just full of lions.

LEO. An old legend.

LEA. Maybe. But suppose all the lions were really there, south of the equator, below the Tropic of Capricorn, and suppose there were a fence that followed the tropic exactly, even along the surface of the ocean. Would you say that the lions were in a cage?

LEO. Absolutely. The space below the Tropic of Capricorn is much smaller than the space above it. And since I said that the cage is always smaller than the rest . . .

LEA. And you agree that the only way to get out of the cage is to cross the fence somehow?

LEO. Absolutely.

LEA. Well, then, suppose the number of lions gets bigger and bigger and bigger, and that the only way to take care of the overcrowding is to shift the fence northward. Then the number of lions gets even bigger, and the fence is moved northward again. This goes on gradually, mile after mile, until the fence ends up being located exactly along the Tropic of Cancer, above the equator. It's a good fence and no lion can cross it. Would you say that the lions were still locked up in a cage?

LEO. Of course.

LEA. Why so? Now the area populated by the lions (below the Tropic of Cancer) is much bigger than the rest of the world (above the tropic). The ratio is perfectly reversed. So either you must accept that all the lions are now *outside*, even though none of them crossed the fence, or you give up your claim that a cage is a small area surrounded by the world.

LEO. But this is just a byproduct of the curvature of the earth . . .

LEA. But the earth *is* round, my dear. And the place we live in is part of the earth. We tend to forget that because we tend to reason on a small scale. But we must think big. Our mind can be a cage, too, and to get out of it we must think like true lions. Otherwise our roaring would be mere pretense, a pathetic exercise, like the Metro-Goldwin-Mayer lion—trapped forever inside a miserable little circle.

REFLECTIONS

HE. Look in the mirror . . . ECNALUBMA is AMBULANCE spelled backward!

SHE. You didn't know that?

HE. I never thought about it. I guess it's spelled backward to make it easy for the drivers to see it in the rear-view mirror.

SHE. Of course, that's the only reason.

HE. Still, it's funny, don't you think?

SHE. What's funny?

HE. That the writing is reversed only along the horizontal axis, not along the vertical one.

SHE. And why should it be otherwise?

HE. I don't know. But I wonder: Why do mirrors reverse right/left but not up/down? Here, take this book on pop music and hold it in front of the mirror. The image of the top part of the title is the top part of the image of the title, but the image of the left part of the title is not the left part of the image of the title. Why? Look at the word *pop*. In the mirror we read *qoq*. Why don't we read *bob* instead?

SHE. Well, hold on a minute. Forget the mirror and take a look at that puddle on the sidewalk right in front of the record store with the big sign. See what happens when the word *pop* is reflected in the puddle? In this case, I read *bob*, not *qoq*. This time, the *p* becomes a *b*, not a *q*: the reversal occurs along the vertical axis, not along the horizontal axis. Are you going to claim that while mirrors reverse right/left but not up/down, puddles reverse up/down but not right/left? How do you explain the difference, given that a puddle is nothing but a mirror lying flat?

HE. Wait a second. Actually, nothing prevents us from seeing the *p* reversed left/right in the puddle too. We just . . . we just have to look at it upside down. Watch me—if I turn my head upside down, the *p* looks again like a *q*, and I read *qoq* in the puddle, too.

SHE. You better keep your head straight and watch out for the traffic! Anyway, if you turn your head upside down to look at a puddle, why don't you do the same thing to look at the mirror? Then the *p* of the book cover becomes a *b*, not a *q*, and you read *bob*. Once you turn yourself upside down, the mirror no longer reverses left/right but only up/down.

HE. I'm still not convinced. I suggested that we look at the puddle upside down because I wanted to adopt the perspective of the puddle people, whose lives are upside down with respect to ours . . .

SHE. But then why don't you do the same with the mirror? Why don't you try to adopt *their* perspective? Since the mirror peoples' lives are reversed left/right with respect to ours, what you take to be a *q* in the mirror is really a *p* from their perspective. So the problem disappears. That's precisely why the people in the mirror can read A M B U L A N C E just like us (though I guess they will have some difficulties with *their* mirrors). If you watch them carefully, when they read, they move their eyes from right to left.

THE MEDDLER, *suddenly showing up in the mirror, signaling with his headlights.* Stop, stop, you're on the wrong track! In the mirror, the only inversion occurs along the front/back axis.

SHE AND HE. Pardon?

THE MEDDLER. If I signal upward, you see me do that in the mirror, too. If my left indicator is flashing, it is flashing on the left of the mirror, too. There is no inversion in either case. But if I want to overtake you, then things change: my image in the mirror comes toward you in the direction opposite to my actual movement. I overtake you from the back, my image from the front. The only real inversion is front/back.

SHE. Oh, come on, you're taking about up/down, left/right, and front/back in a completely different sense, with reference to the external space. You are speaking of absolute directions. We were concerned with the subjective directions.

THE MEDDLER. That's precisely the point. When you say that mirrors reverse right/left but not up/down, you are using the word "reverse" in two different senses.

HE. What should we say, then?

THE MEDDLER. You should say that mirrors always reverse *one* absolute direction, namely, the direction perpendicular to the surface of the mirror. Remember the puddle?

HE. So then, when we look at ourselves in the mirror, the bodily inversion that we see must be an illusion?

THE MEDDLER. It depends on how you position yourself with respect to the front/back direction. If you *stand* in front of the mirror, then your body's left and right are reversed (as are the left and right of any object, such as the letters of the alphabet, that require your body to assume a certain direction—hence *pop* becomes *qoq*). If instead you align yourself along the front/back axis, then it's like being upside down with respect to the surface of the mirror: your body's up and down will be reversed and *pop* will read *bob*.

HE AND SHE. And if we turn sideways?

THE MEDDLER. You must be careful how you phrase that question! But now, excuse me, I must leave your mirror . . . Thanks . . . !ssap ecnalubma eht tel ot revo llup tsum I

It appears that Einstein's job at the Patent Office in Bern, in the years when he was developing the Special Theory of Relativity, was to evaluate various projects concerning the coordination of clocks in Swiss train stations. So does Special Relativity—a truly philosophical chapter in the history of physics—share a bloodline with the logistics of rail transportation? For the skeptical Reader, we have included the letter from Bell-Ringer No. 2353: it is a reminder that in problems of coordination, Time and Space can hardly be kept apart. Granted, there is a big difference between the sound of a bell and the speed of light. But then again, there is a big difference between a humble bell-ringer and Einstein. Nor is this the whole story. Our intuitive concepts of Space and Time are tied to a specific geometry, which is the geometry of everyday objects, and which is responsible for our seeing the Horizon as a flat line in spite of what we have learned in school. As soon as one begins to think big, however, one loses one's bearings on a planet that is not flat but curved. Such intuitive concepts as Birthday, Season, and Inside/Outside don't seem to function anymore. Other concepts, in turn, such as Left and Right or Up and Down, are enough to convert a mirror into a window onto the mixture of the Subjective and the Objective that informs our description of Space as such—a conceptual mixture in which we find ourselves deeply enmeshed and that proves hard to disentangle. That being said, it wouldn't hurt to turn our attention to the objects and events themselves —that is, to those tangible things that reside in Space and Time and of which our concepts are often Abstractions. Which is actually what we are about to do in chapter

5

where a series of seemingly innocent controversies shows how hard it is to count things properly and attribute an Identity to them, to the point that an amoeba no longer knows Who she is, a wise judge is forced to assert that One plus One makes One, an athlete doesn't know how to report his Actions, and a train is liable to Disappear merely because of a lady's thoughtful scruples.

THE LAST CASE OF THE PRESIDENT
OF AMOEBAS

TO THE PRESIDENT OF THE COUNCIL OF THE AMOEBA KINGDOM

DEAR SIR,

I am writing to ask Your High Authority to intervene in a question that has become vitally important to me. Twenty seconds ago, I split off from my immediate ancestral amoeba, M45YY. Actually, *we* split up, since the ancestral amoeba split into two halves. Now, the talk is that about five seconds ago, the *other* half staked her claim to the filiation, and would like to keep the original name M45YY for herself. To avoid any misunderstanding, I request a pronouncement from the Council that will fully acknowledge my rights.

Signed: M45YY

TO THE PRESIDENT OF THE COUNCIL OF THE AMOEBA KINGDOM

DEAR SIR,

I am writing to ask Your High Authority to intervene in a question that has become vitally important to me. Twenty seconds ago, I split off from my immediate ancestral amoeba, M45YY. Actually, *we* split up, since the ancestral amoeba split into two halves. Now, the talk is that about five seconds ago, the *other* half staked her claim to the filiation, and would like to keep the original name M45YY for herself. To avoid any misunderstanding, I request a pronouncement from the Council that will fully acknowledge my rights.

Signed: M45YY

TO THE AMOEBAS TEMPORARILY LABELED M45YY(A)
AND M45YY(B)

DEAR FELLOW AMOEBAS,

Two seconds ago, we received your identical letters simultaneously, each of which stakes a claim to the name M45YY. You may not know it, given your youth, but you can easily imagine that this Council is overburdened with requests of this sort. To be precise, in the ninety-eight minutes of my long career, I have signed one billion, two hundred and thirty million, four hundred twenty thousand, one hundred twenty-seven replies like the one I am now sending you. My suggestion, which is the same suggestion I make in all analogous cases, is that you both accept the temporary name that the Council has automatically assigned to you, as they appear above. In that case, it will suffice that you delete the parentheses at the end of the name. I trust you will accept this solution, and I hope you have no further requests, as I plan to retire in less than three seconds in order to prepare to split apart myself.

Cordially yours,
The President

TO THE PRESIDENT OF THE COUNCIL OF THE AMOEBA KINGDOM

DEAR SIR,

I hereby abide by the policies of the Council, and accept the name assigned to me. Long life to the ectoplasm!

M45YYA

TO THE PRESIDENT OF THE COUNCIL OF THE AMOEBA KINGDOM

DEAR SIR,

I hereby appeal against the policies of the Council, and reject the name assigned to me. Long life to the ectoplasm!

M45YYA

TO M45YY(B)

We regret that we cannot process your appeal, since the procedure expressly requires your signature to correspond to the temporary name you have been assigned by the Council, not to the name claimed by the appellant. But do not worry: if you believe you can produce good reasons in support of your claim, we shall certainly give your appeal all the attention it requires. In the Amoeba Kingdom we attach the highest value to individual opinions!

> *Cordially yours,*
> *The President*

TO THE PRESIDENT OF THE COUNCIL OF THE AMOEBA KINGDOM

DEAR SIR,

It's been six-tenths of a second since my splitting partner and I received your reply, and I already find myself in a situation of great inferiority. The decision to assign the suffix B to my name has proved a serious handicap, in my professional as well as in my personal life. But apart from biographical considerations, my opposition to such a decision stems from a simple observation: there is no reason whatsoever, nor could there be any, to assign the B to my name rather than to the name of my splitting partner. In the absence of a reason, I therefore find the assignment utterly illegitimate. And this has nothing to do with the fact that, whatever the nomenclature, I do find myself wondering who I am.

> *Signed: M45YY ... (I do not accept the B)*

TO M45YY(B)

DEAR FELLOW AMOEBA,

Your observation is an appeal to the Principle of Sufficient Reason. But the import of this principle is *metaphysical* (nothing happens without a reason) and perhaps *epistemological* (if we cannot find any reason why something happened, we should not therefore conclude that it happened without a reason). As regards *normative* issues, our law ruled long ago that the Principle is irrelevant. And *there is a precise reason* behind that ruling. The world of amoebas is very peculiar; it is a "fifty-fifty world." Our biology requires that each amoeba eventually split into two halves, each of which exactly reproduces the immediate ancestral one. Metaphysics forces us to choose the easiest route and to consider that at the time of scission, the ancestral amoeba perishes and two new amoebas come into life. Any other solution would prove either uninteresting or arbitrary. Accordingly, the only distinction on which we can legislate concerns our *names*. We certainly wish to meet with the desires of our fellow amoebas to keep track of their origins, and for this reason, we are happy to grant them the possibility of keeping the name of their immediate ancestor as part of their new name—if they wish to do so. But we cannot go any further except by acting in a purely arbitrary way, and when we assign extensions of names we do so in the only way that our fifty-fifty world allows, which is to say by tossing a coin. Playing heads-or-tails is an utterly respectable practice in our world, and it makes no sense to complain about the outcome by appealing to the Principle of Sufficient Reason. Nor would it be legitimate to complain because the toss was performed against the wind, or because the tossing officer had dirty fingers, or because the coin had been in the hands of a child, or what have you. In a fifty-fifty world, such factors are totally irrelevant.

As I have already said, I am about to retire, and I will not have time to examine any further questions you might have. I kindly ask you, therefore, to accept the name that you have been assigned. In case you do wish to plead your case further, I can only invite you to write to one or the other—your choice—of the two amoebas that will take my place.

Cordially yours,
The President

THE HIDDEN STATUE

HE, *dragging a huge granite block through the door.* Look what I bought!

SHE. A cube?

HE. A statue. We'll put it right here in the entrance.

SHE. Finally, a piece of contemporary art. Very elegant—almost minimalist. But I thought you would only go for something much more classical . . .

HE. Let's say it's a compromise between classicism and modernity; a modern play on a classical icon. This cube contains a faithful reproduction of Michelangelo's *David* (on a small scale, of course).

SHE. You mean that this thing is a box? What a fine idea: I've never seen a box made of granite.

HE. No, there's no opening. It's not a box. The cube is solid, with no moving parts. But inside this cube there is a part shaped exactly like Michelangelo's *David*.

SHE. A part shaped exactly like Michelangelo's *David?* What's so special about that? This cucumber has a part shaped exactly like Michelangelo's *David* too (on a smaller scale). And also a part shaped exactly like the *Venus de Milo*, for that matter. And a part shaped like the *Venus* with the *David* on top of it.

HE. So what? The farmer is not an artist. The author of this statue, by contrast, is a renowned artist. He has made a series of ten reproductions of famous works. The series is special precisely because the reproductions are hidden inside, completely enclosed within a thick layer of matter, specifically, by a layer of the same matter of which the statue is made. This one is made of granite and the layer is fashioned so as to form a cube. But there were also statues made of marble and others made of clay. And they came in many fashions: sphere-shaped, cone-shaped, pyramid-shaped . . .

SHE. And *David*-shaped? I mean, why not also a reproduction of Michelangelo's *David* surrounded by a layer shaped like *David?*

HE. Pardon?

SHE. Oh dear, they fooled you once again. How could you believe the layer story? They gave you a block of granite and made you pay a fortune for it. A part hidden inside a block of granite is not a statue, even though it may be shaped like one.

HE. But if it is shaped like Michelangelo's *David*, why is it not a *David*?

SHE. It is not a *David* because it is not *yet* a *David*. It would become one if the artist brought it to light by removing what you call the surrounding layer. At that point we would say that that piece of granite—that portion of the cube that is now hidden inside—is a statue. But so far, we only have a part surrounded by another. Nothing more than a big granite cube.

HE. Sorry, but don't the artist's intentions mean anything to you?

SHE. Your cube is more like Michelangelo's *Prisoners* than like his *David*. Even if we took the artist's intentions into account, this is at best an incomplete work.

HE. It seems pretty complete to me. Look at it—what a perfect cube. I'm thrilled at the thought of my *David* hidden inside it. And I am sure my *David* is perfectly complete too: There are no missing pieces.

SHE. Let's see. How many parts inside this cube are shaped like Michelangelo's *David*?

HE. Let me think . . .

SHE. I'll tell you how many—lots of them! To begin with, imagine a part shaped like *David*. Now imagine another part inside the first, but a little smaller. And now another, smaller part . . . Or imagine a part that has exactly the same size and shape as the first, but located one inch to the left. Or one inch to the right. And so on. *Which* of those parts is the one that your artist is supposed to have "sculpted"? *Which* of those "statues" have you bought?

THE MEDDLER, *entering without knocking, dressed like a mailman; on closer inspection, nose and mustache seem to be fake.* May I come in?

HE. Be my guest. You've already done so anyway.

THE MEDDLER. You've forgotten the booklet that comes with your artwork, sir. May I read? "This block of granite contains a five-inch part shaped like Michelangelo's *David*, located twenty inches from the bottom, centered, with the head facing the north side of the cube. This is my sculpture, entitled *Hommage to Michelangelo*. Signed: the Artist."

HE. Five inches, you said? Well, I thought it was a bit bigger . . . With all this granite around it . . .

SHE. Your artist is smart: he certainly knows how to use his brain, if not his arm. But did I get it right—The head facing the *north* side?

HE. Apparently. But which one is the north side of the cube? It doesn't say anywhere. This is a perfectly polished cube, with no marks whatsoever.

THE MEDDLER. I suppose the north side is the side that will face north once you have decided where to put the cube.

HE. Of course! That way we also get to play an active role in the making of the statue. I like this artist more and more.

SHE. And if none of the sides face north? What if we put the cube at an angle—would your statue cease to exist?

THE MEDDLER. Correct. The statue exists only when one of the sides faces north.

HE. What an ingenious piece of work. Sometimes it exists, sometimes it doesn't. And if we rotate the cube, every time a new side stands facing north, a new *David*-shaped part will correspond to the artist's instructions. Our statue changes continuously, like a Calder mobile.

SHE. But how do we know that it is one statue that changes? Think about it. When side 1 stands facing north, there is a statue of *David*. When side 2 stands facing north, there is a statue of *David*. But how do we know whether it is the same statue or a different one?

THE MEDDLER, *carefully scrutinizing both sides of the booklet*. Here it doesn't say.

HE. If the artist doesn't say anything explicit, we are free to decide. I find this quite original, too.

SHE. I would say it is always a different statue, since it is made of different matter.

HE. I'd rather think it is always the same statue—a statue that materializes in different parts of the cube.

SHE. You are deceiving yourself. Michelangelo's *Prisoners* don't give you all this leeway, and that's the reason we may speak of them as statues imprisoned inside the rock. They are incomplete, but in a way, they have an identity of their own. Your *David*, by contrast, exists only in your mind.

HE. We can still speculate: What would the *Prisoners* be like had Michelangelo completed his work?

SHE. That's an interesting question for a conceptual artist, I must admit. But not for a lazy artist like yours.

A CUPBOARD IN PIECES

JUDGE. Who wants to speak first?

MRS. SMITH. I do, Your Honor! A few days ago, I went to Mr. Jones's furniture store and purchased a cupboard, paying the full amount in cash— one thousand dollars. Now he refuses to deliver the furniture!

MR. JONES. I'm not delivering it yet because the payment is not complete.

SMITH. Don't be silly! I gave you the money personally and you signed a receipt. Here it is, Your Honor . . .

JONES. Your Honor, may I say something? I'm not denying that Mrs. Smith gave me a thousand dollars. That's the amount corresponding to the price of the cupboard. But she still owes me another thousand dollars for the pieces that compose the cupboard. The total, therefore, amounts to two thousand dollars.

JUDGE. I'm not sure I follow you. If the price of the cupboard is one thousand dollars, and if that is the amount paid by Mrs. Smith, why are you asking for another thousand?

SMITH, *grumbling*. That's exactly my point!

JONES. Let me explain. We can't deliver the cupboard without at the same time delivering all the pieces that compose it, right? For this reason, we would never consider selling it without also selling the pieces. On this point we have always been crystal clear, and our customers have never complained: whoever buys some furniture must buy all the pieces that come with it, and vice versa.

SMITH. Your customers have never complained because they never realized they were being ripped off. It's obviously a fraud, and I am not going to fall for it . . .

JUDGE, *to Jones*. Actually your explanation is puzzling. Why do you want to draw a distinction between a cupboard and the set of pieces that compose it? Isn't the set of pieces *just the same* as the cupboard?

JONES. If you will allow me, Your Honor, the cupboard and the set of pieces that compose it have different properties. Thus, by Leibniz's Law—which says that this and that are the same thing only if this and that are perfectly alike in every respect—the cupboard and the set of pieces that compose it are not the same thing. For instance, you will agree that if I took the pieces apart and delivered them to Mrs. Smith, she would have good reason to complain.

SMITH. Of course I would!

JONES. The reason is that once the pieces are taken apart, the cupboard ceases to exist. But the pieces are all there, so the set of pieces continues to exist. We must therefore conclude that we are dealing with *two* entities, only one of which (the set of pieces) survives disassembly. There are two entities, but we make a point of never selling them separately. We do the same with all our furniture, and we're proud of it. We're aware that our competition is willing to sell the pieces in a box, leaving it to the customer to assemble them. We don't like that kind of service. Now, in the case at issue, it so happens that one thing—the cupboard—costs one thousand dollars and the other—the set of pieces—costs another thousand dollars. So the total amounts to two thousand.

JUDGE. Let me get this straight. You're saying that the cupboard is distinct from the set of pieces that compose it insofar as their properties are distinct.

JONES. Right. Their survival conditions are distinct. Here is another example: the cupboard is in a very specific style—Biedermeier—but the individual pieces don't have any style.

JUDGE. I understand that. What I don't understand is why you stop there. Besides the cupboard and the set of pieces that compose it, you could distinguish many other things at this point. For instance, all the pieces that compose the cupboard could be cut in half, right? Hence, besides the set of pieces that compose the cupboard (the drawers, the shelves, the panels, and what have you), we also have the set of their halves—let's say the right and left halves of each piece. According to your reasoning, once the pieces are cut in half, they go out of existence, but their halves would continue to exist—hence the set of pieces and the set of their halves have different "survival conditions." Am I wrong?

JONES. On the contrary, Your Honor, you're perfectly right. I never thought about it . . . Let me make a note of this.

JUDGE. Hold on and listen to me. It would appear, then, that we must make a distinction between the cupboard, the set of its pieces, and the set of its half-pieces. But this is just the beginning. Each piece can be cut in many ways: into the right and left halves, into the top and bottom halves, into the front and back halves, into three equal parts, into four equal parts, and so on and so forth. Should we conclude that each possible way of cutting the pieces yields a different entity, a different set of things that compose the cupboard?

JONES. Actually . . . this is really interesting. (*Keeps writing while trying to listen to the judge.*)

JUDGE. And each one of those entities would have its price?

JONES, *pondering.* Well, I . . .

JUDGE. Mr. Jones, it is obvious that by this pattern, your cupboard would cost a fortune.

SMITH, *still grumbling.* And they call it a sale . . .

JONES. I'm sorry, Your Honor. But if you agree with me that it is not enough to have the pieces to have a cupboard, you must also agree that it isn't enough to have the pieces cut in half, or the pieces cut into a hundred parts . . .

JUDGE. I do agree with all that. What I am questioning is your claim that such conceptual distinctions entail a real distinction. Conceptually, there is a big difference between me as a person and me as a judge. And it's true: the day I retire, Judge Williams will no longer exist, whereas Mary Williams will continue to exist, at least for a while. But this is no reason to claim that, at this moment in time, two distinct people are sitting on this chair—Judge Williams and Mary Williams.

JONES. Well, in a way . . .

JUDGE. But don't you see the sophistry? It's obvious to everybody that there is just one person sitting on this chair, a person who can be designated or described in different ways. The names and descriptions by means of which one can refer to me can vary as time goes by, and some descriptions may also cease to be adequate while others still apply, but this is of little consequence. Likewise, some pieces of wood can be arranged in such a way as to compose a cupboard, or those pieces can be cut into a bunch of small fragments. In the first case, it would be correct to describe the set of pieces as a cupboard; in the second case, it would not. But this doesn't allow you to say that we are dealing with two distinct *things*. The cupboard is nothing over and above the sum of its pieces arranged in a certain way. And whoever buys the cupboard buys the pieces *arranged that way*. That's why the buyer would be entitled to complain if you delivered the pieces disassembled. If you want to charge one thousand dollars for the cupboard and one thousand dollars for the set of pieces, go ahead. But when you prepare the bill, remember that the total amounts to one thousand dollars, because there is *just one thing* that you are charging for. The case is closed.

HOLTER MONITOR

SHE. Strange apparatus you have there. It looks like a CD player, but I see cables that go under your shirt . . . What is it?

HE. It's a Holter monitor: it registers the electric activity of my heart. Very useful for sporting people like me. Today, for example, I went cycling for about twenty miles, with several steep climbs, and all of my heartbeats are recorded here, one by one. Now I can use these data to prepare for my next workout. Scientific training, you know . . .

SHE. And how can you access the data?

HE. It's all in this memory card. You can remove it and insert it into a laptop, and the screen will show you a detailed diagram. Actually, since I'm done with my twenty-four hour cycle, let me show you . . . Here, see, these are my heartbeats at 12:30 p.m. . . . . I was resting, so not much activity. But here I must have been going uphill, since my heart rate is up to 130. Let me check . . . Yes, at 2:20 p.m., I was cycling up a steep climb.

SHE. You remember everything you've done during the day?

HE. I kept a diary, of course. Pretty detailed, I must say: they gave me precise instructions.

SHE. So by checking your diary, you can now establish a connection between your cardiac activity and your bodily movements. Interesting. It's like having a detailed photograph of the functioning of your heart, with a clear indication of the causes underlying each change.

HE. Exactly.

SHE. Still . . .

HE. What?

SHE. Can I see your diary? There's nothing personal in it, I hope.

HE. Not at all. Here it is.

SHE. Let's see . . . From 10 a.m. to 10:20 a.m. you are sitting at your desk. At 10:20, you get up and go to the kitchen to eat a croissant. At 10:25, you go back to your desk, until 10:55. Fine: three time intervals, three actions. But now look here. At 10:55 a.m. you go out to buy another croissant, and you come back at 11:15. You count this as a fourth action. But it seems to me that there is a big difference between going to the kitchen to eat a croissant and going to the bakery to buy a croissant. In the latter case, you are bound to do many other things: you exit the apartment, go down the stairs, walk for two blocks, enter the bakery, ask for a croissant, wait for your turn at the cashier, get the money out of your wallet, pay, and so on. Why should all of this count as one single action?

HE. I see your point. But then the same reasoning would apply to the croissant in the kitchen, wouldn't it? I get up, walk toward the kitchen, open the cupboard, grab the croissant, lift it to my lips, bite it . . . Many actions, not one.

SHE. Right. So what determines *how many* actions you have performed?

HE. I suppose I confined myself to classifying my actions on the basis of what I thought was particularly significant at that moment.

SHE. So we could say that there is some important action that is the goal of your activity, and that that action "dominates" all the others—it "trumps" them.

HE. Yes, that's roughly the criterion I used: I paid attention to those actions that were most salient. I tried to make a note of the ones that I thought could result in an acceleration of my cardiac activity, even though it is very likely that I missed many of them. When you go cycling, you often speed up and then slow down, and I certainly did not record each such change. On the other hand, as you pointed out, I made a note when I got up from my desk to get a croissant. Perhaps, given that I had been sitting in the same place for a long time, the transition to the kitchen struck me as important. Perhaps we use different criteria to classify our actions depending on when and where we perform them?

SHE. There are psychological studies about the way in which we subdivide actions into smaller sequences. It appears that language plays a significant role: we have words for some actions and not for others, and we analyze our doings in terms of those actions that we can name.

HE. The American artist Kenneth Goldsmith has published a diary in which he registered every single action he performed during a day. For example, not just eating a croissant, but also raising your arm, lifting it to your lips . . .

SHE. *Every* single action? I don't believe it.

HE. Why not?

SHE. Think about it. You have just eaten your croissant. As planned, you must now write down that you have eaten a croissant. But if your goal is to make a note of every single action, then you must go on and write that you have written down that you have eaten a croissant. And immediately afterwards, you must write that (1) you have written that (2) you have written that (3) you have eaten a croissant. And so on forever.

HE. Point taken. But this is not to say that I cannot make a note of every action I perform. As a matter of fact, if I went on like that, at the end of the day I *would* have written down every action I had performed, namely, that I have written that I have written that I have written . . . who knows how many times? After all, that's all I would have done for the whole day, after eating my croissant. The real problem strikes me as different. I have written that I have eaten a croissant. At this point, why should I write that I have written the sentence "I have eaten a croissant"? I could also write that I have written the word "I," then the word "have," then the word "eaten," and so on. And then I could write that I have written that I have written "I," and that I have written "have," and that I have written "eaten," and so on forever.

SHE. Why should you describe what you have done in terms of words rather than sentences?

HE. There's no reason, that's the point. Of course, I could also describe what I have done letter by letter: I have written "I," then "h," then "a," . . . There just isn't a *right way* to describe the action of my writing that I have eaten a croissant. There is no "good" description of what I have done. This ought to paralyze me immediately!

SHE. Right. So the task of keeping track of every action performed in a day is impossible. One cannot determine the exact number of all the actions one performs, just as one cannot determine the exact number of all the objects that one sees in a room.

HE. But the Holter test doesn't require one to write down *every* action. From a medical perspective, one need not be so fine-grained.

SHE. Then let us say that those who take the test should be given precise instructions: *how* fine-grained is the description of his or her day supposed to be?

ROW 13

STEWARD'S VOICE. Fasten your seat belts.

PASSENGER. Good morning. Sorry to bother you, but that's my seat. 14A. I always choose a window seat—even on long flights.

HE. You said it—this is a long flight. Too long for my taste; I always feel a bit uneasy when I fly. Call it superstition, but at least we're not sitting in row 13!

PASSENGER. I don't mean to make you nervous, but this *is* row 13.

HE. What? We're not in row 14?

PASSENGER. "14" is the number written on the seats. But look at the number on the seats in front of us.

HE. 12! We are sitting behind row 12! So we are sitting in row 13 even though the tag says "14." I don't like this. I am going to change my seat . . .

PASSENGER. If you want to change your seat, it means you are a Platonist. You believe that numbers exist and are what they are independently of what we call them, right?

HE. I don't know whether I'm a Platonist, but I *am* superstitious. And if this is the row behind row 12, something tells me that we are seated precisely in the row I don't want to be in, regardless of what they call it. Really, I feel cheated: if it weren't for you, I would have been under the false impression of being seated in the fourteenth row.

PASSENGER. On the other hand, perhaps there is nothing to worry about, even if you are superstitious. Perhaps there *was* a thirteenth row, but they removed it, and then reduced the space between the twelfth and the fourteenth rows. Perhaps this company has a hangar somewhere where they keep all the thirteenth rows of their aircraft.

HE. Or perhaps they put them all in a movie theater . . . I seriously doubt that they would do anything so complicated and expensive just to please their superstitious customers. Probably all they do is erase a numeral, pretending it's like erasing a number. A philosophical fraud.

PASSENGER. Indeed. I'm surprised nobody has ever complained.

HE. Besides, if the problem were just the numeral, they could have left the thirteenth row where it is, changing only the name—as in "row 12B," or "Unnumbered Row." Isn't that what they do in Manhattan, where people don't like living on the thirteenth floor?

PASSENGER. Well, I'm actually involved in the project for the "Multi-Culture Tower." I don't know if you have heard about it—it's going to be a 300-story skyscraper . . .

HE. The new tower of Babel!

PASSENGER. You have no idea of how many problems of this sort we had to face. The Americans don't want the thirteenth floor; the Italians don't want the seventeenth. We'll have to skip the third, the seventh, the forty-eighth, and many more: every culture has its own superstitions. And that's just the beginning. The Americans start counting from the ground floor, so they call it the first floor; for the Europeans the ground floor is just floor zero, since they start counting from the next. So we'll also have to skip the fourteenth floor, the eighteenth, and so on.

HE. But how can you "skip" a floor? Are you just renaming it, as they did with our seats?

PASSENGER. No. We did a survey, and it turns out that seventy percent of the world's population is Platonist, just like you. So in the end we have decided to leave a gap—an open space, an architectural hole. Seen from a distance, our tower will look like a lace curtain.

HE. You should rename your tower the "Lace of Superstition." I understand it must be very difficult to make everybody happy. Perhaps this is why superstition is more about the symbols than about the things themselves. Anyway, I must admit this conversation made me a bit nervous. Let us see what the music program has to offer. Here . . . Mahler's *Lied von der Erde*. That's just perfect—very relaxing.

PASSENGER. An unfortunate coincidence, if I may say so. You are forgetting that to avoid the fate of those composers who only managed to live long enough to compose nine symphonies—Beethoven and Schubert, for example—upon completing his *Lied von der Erde*, Mahler decided to consider it a symphony—the one following his eighth—and hastened to compose one more symphony and about half of yet another . . .

HE. The ones we call the ninth and the tenth? Then we should call them the tenth and the eleventh. Good grief—a superstition can really be worthless if we don't pay attention to the difference between numbers and numerals!

PASSENGER. Except that the trick didn't work. As it turned out, Gustav Mahler passed away before his Ninth was played in public for the first time.

TRAIN CANCELLED

ANNOUNCER, *over the loudspeaker.* Attention please. The 5:02 train, final destination Rome, has been cancelled. We apologize for any inconvenience.

HE, *to himself.* Darn, that *is* an inconvenience. I thought I could make it in time for dinner. But it's always the same story with these trains—you can *never* make plans!

LADY. This cancellation worries me. I wonder, what did they do to the 5:02 train?

HE. What do you mean?

LADY. The announcement said it had been cancelled.

HE. I heard that, which is why I am upset. Are you also going to Rome?

LADY. I am. But that's not the point. I love trains, and the thought that they've cancelled one gives me the shivers. I wonder what happened to it: was it demolished? Or burned? Or buried?

HE. Excuse me, but you don't really think that they did away with an actual, concrete train made of locomotives and carriages, do you?

LADY. What else could they have cancelled? As far as I know, every train is made of locomotives, carriages, seats, windows, and so on. Those are *concrete* things, you know. I have never had the pleasure of traveling on an *abstract* train. Thus, if they say that the 5:02 train has been cancelled, I figure they have done away with a locomotive and a number of carriages, seats, windows, and so on. And I get worried.

HE. Then you are what philosophers call a nominalist. You only believe in the existence of concrete things.

LADY. Do you think there are also abstract trains?

HE. Of course. Our language allows us to speak of concrete things, such as the train that is now approaching on track 9, as well as abstract things, such as the train that is due to arrive on track 9 every day at this time. A concrete train can suffer a mechanical failure, but when they cancel a train, they do not destroy a concrete train—they just cancel an abstract train. They suppress a certain *type* of train.

LADY. If you think that a cancelled train is an abstract entity, then you must be worried, too. If the 5:02 train has been cancelled in your sense, it means that at 5:02 there will never be another train to Rome. Never.

HE. Let me rephrase that. What is being cancelled is an event of a certain type: the departure of the 5:02 train with final destination Rome.

LADY. I'm not sure I'm following you. A train is not an event, is it? It is something made of iron, wood, and other solid stuff. In any case, are you talking about a concrete event or an abstract event? To put it differently, do you often take a 5:02 train to Rome?

HE. Every Friday, to go back to my family.

LADY. You must admit, though, that each time counts as a different event. So you must agree that the entity they have suppressed, if it was an event, could not be an abstract entity. In a way, it must have been a concrete thing—a unique, unrepeatable token. If we had left yesterday at 5:02 p.m., that would have been a different event. It would have been a different departure.

HE. Do you often take the 5:02 train?

LADY. I keep a very detailed diary and can give you a precise record. Let's see. Last Friday, I took a train that left at 5:02 p.m. Two Fridays ago, I took a train that left at 5:02 p.m. Three Fridays ago . . .

HE. All right, I can see your nominalism is pretty solid, like the trains on which you travel. You really don't want to say that you often take *the* 5:02 train to Rome, as I would put it. But how can you stick to this way of speaking? How can you avoid all reference to abstract types? Do you always use such long lists of concrete objects and particular events?

LADY. I have no trouble saying that I take "the same train" every Friday, if that makes you happy. But just as a manner of speaking. Like when I complain that my friends always cook "the same meals": I obviously do not mean to say that they cook the same meals over and over . . .

ANNOUNCER, *over the loudspeaker.* Attention please. Train 819 with final destination Rome will depart at 5:45 rather than 5:02. We apologize for any inconvenience.

HE. Did you hear that? They must have solved the problem.

LADY. I hope you are right, but how can you be so sure? Perhaps our train has already been cancelled (*sighs*), and now they are telling us to take this other train . . .

THE MEDDLER. Excuse me. I am not a nominalist, but I must say I agree with the lady. How can we be sure that this is the same train, meaning the abstract train this gentleman was talking about?

HE. I beg your pardon?

THE MEDDLER. How can it be the 5:02 train if it leaves at 5:45?

HE. They announced it as train 819. And that is the number of the train that was supposed to leave at 5:02. They announced it as train 819 because that is the name of our train.

THE MEDDLER. Forget the name (otherwise we all become nominalists). The problem is the named entity: is it really the same train? After all, it lacks one of the main properties that characterized our train (the property of leaving at 5:02 p.m.). Think about it: if this train now makes a few more stops, will it be the same train? What if it leaves with fewer carriages than planned? What if it leaves from a different track?

HE. As far as I'm concerned, the fact that a train leaves forty-three minutes late means nothing. Indeed, I don't think the 5:02 train to Rome has *ever* left at 5:02 sharp.

THE MEDDLER. Note, however, that we would not feel so easy with the thought that a train can leave forty-three minutes early. We wouldn't really say that it was the same train.

HE. But no train ever leaves earlier than scheduled . . .

THE MEDDLER. Then suppose that, for some reason, the 819 train to Rome leaves exactly twenty-four hours later, at 5:02 *tomorrow*. You wouldn't say that it was the same train, would you?

HE. How would I know? Ask this lady. As far as I can tell, if they announce it as the 5:02 train to Rome, then it is the 5:02 train to Rome, regardless of when it actually leaves and where it leaves from.

LADY. What an odd thing to say. Surely the identity of a train is defined by the identity of the carriages, seats, windows, and the other things of which it is made.

THE MEDDLER. To me, you both sound odd. Never mind concrete trains or abstract trains. You should do what I do: I always take the bus.

SATELLITES

SHE. Listen to this: "What is a concept? As a first approximation, a concept is what determines a class of objects—a class that can in principle contain a single element. (For instance, the concept *satellite of Earth* determines a class with just one element, the Moon.)"

HE. What did you just say? The Earth only has one satellite?

SHE. Of course. There are planets, like Jupiter, that have more, but the Earth's only satellite is the Moon.

HE. You're forgetting all those artificial satellites.

SHE. I see. In a way you're right—they too qualify as terrestrial satellites. Perhaps the author of this book should have written that the concept *natural satellite of the Earth* determines a class with just one element. That would have been uncontroversial, since the Moon is the only natural satellite . . .

THE MEDDLER, *who, running by, hears her last few words and makes an abrupt stop.* Absolutely not! There are many more than that, madam. I work for a company that has just put twenty-four new natural satellites into orbit.

SHE. So what? If they have been put into orbit by your company, then they are not *natural* satellites . . . There are now twenty-four more satellites orbiting around our planet, but the Moon is still the only natural one.

THE MEDDLER. Nonsense! Our satellites are nothing but rocks that we took from a river located in a deserted area. We put a lot of care in choosing them so that they would qualify as natural by all standards.

SHE. What a curious idea! Why did you put those rocks into orbit, if I may ask?

THE MEDDLER. It's a piece of conceptual art. Our rocks are now in geostationary orbit, and as they enter or exit the night zone (the shadow of our planet), they give us the time. Every hour, a different satellite becomes visible in the sky.

SHE. Very original and poetic. But in spite of what you're saying, your satellites are and remain artificial.

THE MEDDLER. Why so? If I picked up one of these stones and put it down over there, would I thereby make it into an artificial thing?

SHE. Of course not. Moving a stone a few feet does not change it in any significant way. But if you did something else with it, for instance, if you carved it into a statue . . . There is no question that a statue is an artifact, something artificial.

HE. I agree. There are philosophers who maintain that a marble statue is nothing but a piece of marble shaped in a certain fashion. But even so, both statue and stone (after the carving) would qualify as artificially modified objects.

THE MEDDLER. Consider those artists who work with *objets trouvés*. Sometime they just take a certain object—a stone, a feather—remove it from its natural location, and put it in a different place—a museum, say— where it becomes a work of art. Sometime, moving an object is *all* it takes to create a work of art . . .

SHE. Sometimes it is, yes.

THE MEDDLER. But that doesn't mean that we end up with an artificial object. Suppose a conceptual artist invites her friends for an evening party on her terrace and says, pointing at the Moon: "For the next twenty seconds the Moon will be part of my new creation." You may want to say that the Moon becomes a work of *art*. But you are not going to say that by doing so our artist is transforming the Moon into something *artificial*—are you?

SHE. Surely not. Our artist would have to do something material to the Moon. It is what you did with your rocks that makes the difference. Our artist did not put the Moon into orbit, whereas you did exactly that with your rocks: you took them from the river and sent them into the sky. That is why I say they are artificial satellites.

THE MEDDLER. According to Aristotle, if you throw a stone in the air, it begins to fall because it tries to reach its natural place, which is the ground. The theory you are presupposing is very Aristotelian. Do you think there is a natural place for everything? If we apply this idea to the case at issue, we end up saying that throwing a stone in the air is enough to make it into an artificial object.

SHE. I didn't say that your rocks are artificial *objects*. I said they are artificial *satellites*. There's a big difference.

HE. I agree. Those are two different concepts. But I wouldn't say that those rocks are artificial satellites, either. Our concept of an artificial satellite is very specific: it picks out a class of objects that are typically made of metal, they are round-shaped, they have antennas, small propellers, and so on. Some things of that kind never make it into orbit, yet they qualify as artificial satellites.

THE MEDDLER. I can assure you that our twenty-four satellites have nothing in common with those horrible contraptions!

SHE. All right, I concede that the concept of an artificial satellite is not easily broken down into its basic features. There are artificial satellites that are not satellites, like those that stay on the ground, and there are satellites that are not artificial satellites even though they are put into orbit by artificial means, like your rocks.

HE. So those rocks are neither artificial objects nor artificial satellites.

SHE. Right. But this is not to say that they are natural satellites. On the contrary, I still firmly believe they're not: they are satellites and they are natural, but that's it. The Earth still has just one natural satellite— the Moon.

Our Reader will appreciate the stubborn obstinacy of certain Metaphysics: after all this time, it still tends to inflict its putative problems on us. The One and the Many have been the greatest source of anguish in Philosophy. Go for the One and you lose track of the differences among things; go for the Many and you lose track of their similarities. Once we put it like that, it certainly appears to be a deep conundrum, and it comes as no surprise that so many books have been written in an effort to untangle it—books that are sometimes very hard to read. Our short parables—concerning not only living (and humble) creatures such as amoebas but also inanimate things such as furniture, trains, events, and works of art—aim at no solution. But the Reader will see the point behind it all. For what looks like a metaphysical conundrum may very well be a linguistic predicament. Sometimes making a choice between the One and the Many depends on how we describe things, as the Judge reminds us. She is One, in spite of having Two different names. And the lesson of the Meddler's otherwise admirable project to send a bunch of rocks into orbit is that coming up with names that adequately reflect our conceptions of things may itself be a difficult matter. Which takes us straight to chapter

6

in which what one Says is carefully weighed up, and where the Meddler demonstrates, contrary to standard lore, that a Word may be worth a thousand Pictures, not a Picture a thousand Words; and in which a capricious pen cap provides the background for a not-so-idle controversy on the difficulties involved in compiling a Dictionary.

VERBATIM

CLERK. Good morning, sir. May I help you?

HE. Good morning. I was walking by and I saw your request.

CLERK. What request?

HE. To enter through this door.

CLERK. Pardon me?

HE. There is a sign on your window that says: "Use the entrance on 113th Street." This is the entrance on 113th Street, isn't it?

CLERK. Oh, yes, I'm sorry, I didn't understand what you were talking about. The store is undergoing renovation and the entrance on Broadway is temporarily closed. Sorry for the inconvenience. So, what can I do for you?

HE. I don't know! Just go ahead and tell me why you wanted me to use this entrance.

CLERK. As I was saying, our entrance on Broadway is temporarily out of service . . .

HE. Listen, you've already said that, and I understand what you said. What I don't understand—what you've not explained to me—is why you ask people like me to use the entrance on 113th Street. I don't have that much time, so I would really appreciate it if you could skip the apologies and just tell me what you want from me.

CLERK, *confounded but still composed*. We don't want anything from anybody. The sign is for those who wish to pay us a visit. If you do not wish to do so then you don't have to do it; that's understood.

HE. If the sign is only intended for certain people, why don't you say so explicitly? Why don't you put up a sign that says: "Those who wish to pay a visit to Castoldi & Bros are kindly invited to use the entrance on 113th

Street," or something like that. One reads the sign and decides what to do. I, for one, did not wish to pay a visit to this store—I didn't even know it existed—so I would not have felt compelled to enter. But your actual sign is more straightforward. It says: "Use the entrance on 113th Street." That's an imperative, so I assumed I was supposed to enter. Anybody would.

CLERK. I'm sorry, sir, but don't you think that some things can be taken for granted? Are you telling me that you pull open every door that says "Pull," or that you start to walk whenever you see a traffic light that says "Walk"?

HE. What do you mean? If I see a sign that says "Pull," then I pull. Why shouldn't I? Whatever the sign refers to, I pull it—a door, a string, a fire alarm . . . whatever. Why would anybody put up a sign that says "Pull" if they don't want people to pull?

CLERK. Let me explain, sir. A sign is a sign insofar as it is meant to convey a message. And generally speaking, the interpretation of a message presupposes a certain sense of relevance on the part of the addressee. Certainly this is the case of those signs that say "Pull" or "Walk" or "Use the entrance next door." Those are not imperatives to be blindly followed. They are to be understood *cum grano salis*. "Be relevant!" According to the philosopher Paul Grice, this is one of the most fundamental rules underlying successful conversation, and I would say that it applies to every form of communication—including door and street signs.

HE. I don't know what you're talking about. If the sign says "Pull," I pull.

CLERK. Sir, may I also remind you of the other fundamental Gricean maxims? Besides the maxim of relevance, there are three more: (a) the maxim of *quantity*—make your contribution as informative as is required for the current purposes of the exchange; (b) the maxim of *quality*—do not say what you believe to be false, and do not say that for which you lack adequate evidence; and (c) the maxim of *manner*—be perspicuous, and specifically avoid ambiguity, obscurity of expression, and unnecessary prolixity.

HE. This is getting to be too much! If I were not in a rush, I would demand to speak to your boss. But this is your lucky day—I don't have any time to waste. I have to rush to the train station.

CLERK, *relieved*. Going out of town for a nice weekend?

HE. I have no idea. I've just read the paper. It says that the airports are all closed and that everybody must take the train.

THE INTELLIGENT DICTIONARY

FROM: READING COMMITTEE

DEAR EDITORIAL BOARD,

We have carefully examined the manuscript of Professor Pocheparole's *The Intelligent Dictionary* and we have no hesitation in recommending it for publication. This is a brilliant book—elegant, compact, devoid of useless sciolisms, and above all, immune from the so-called circularity problem. Here are our reasons.

Many dictionaries contain definitions that go in a circle. For instance, the one we commonly use defines "action" as "the process or state of acting," and defines "to act" as "to carry out an action." If you want to find out what an action is, you have to know the answer already. Such definitions are circular and, therefore, devoid of any informative content. True, not every word is defined in this way. For instance, we have not yet found a dictionary in which "dog" is defined as a human's best friend and "human" as an entity whose best friend is a dog. Nonetheless, circularities are frequent, and anybody who is logically trained and keen on precision will find them utterly vicious. Besides, enlarging a circle does not make it less vicious. We can define "action" as "what an agent does," "agent" as "an individual who acts," and "to act" as "to carry out an action," and we are still stuck in a circle. We suspect that this is exactly how dictionaries work: they disguise the circularity of their definitions by enlarging the circles. But that does not solve the problem.

Now, Professor Pocheparole's idea is simply ingenious. Let us leave out—she says—all those word that need no definition, i.e., those words that are so common that everybody knows their meaning. Then let us define the other words in terms of the ones that we have left out. This will avoid all circularities. For example, if we define "action" as "what a person does" we are left with "person." Since everybody knows what "person" means, there is no need to include a definition for this word. And since nobody will look for this word anyway, we can just leave it out of the dictionary. It's as simple as Columbus's egg.

FROM: MARKETING DEPARTMENT

DEAR EDITORIAL BOARD,

We strongly advise against the publication of Professor Pocheparole's so-called *Intelligent Dictionary*. Just imagine how our readers would react as soon as they realized that the dictionary contains no entry whatsoever for such important words as "person," "dog," or "heaven." What dictionary can afford such gaps? We are not lexicographers, but to us it seems obvious that a dictionary *must* be circular. A dictionary in which words do not go in a circle is bound to be useless: circularity may raise a theoretical issue, but in practice it is perfectly all right. It's not a drawback—it's a plus.

PS: By the way, what is "Columbus's egg"? We looked for a definition in the manuscript, but we couldn't find any.

FROM: PROFESSOR POCHEPAROLE

DEAR EDITORIAL BOARD,

Thank you for passing along the comments of the Reading Committee and of the Marketing Department. May I propose a compromise? Let us include all words, but let us not give any definition for the most common ones, whose meaning is already known to everybody. This will suffice to steer clear of the circularity problem.

PS: I have a beautiful, handmade sewing egg from Columbia right in front of me. I'd be happy to pass it to the Marketing Department. In some cases, *showing* is much better than defining!

FROM: EDITORIAL BOARD

"Columbus's egg" (not "Columbian") is not something you can find in a dictionary, just as you cannot find "Columbus." A dictionary is not an encyclopedia or a phone book, so it cannot contain proper names and definite descriptions. Its purpose is to define concepts, not to catalog objects. And this much should be obvious: Columbus's egg was an object, just as Achilles' heel and Pandora's box were.

TO: CUSTOMER SERVICE

I would like to return the copy of your *Intelligent Dictionary* that I have just purchased. I have looked in vain for the meaning of the expression "Columbus's egg," which according to my older brothers stands for a concept I should get better acquainted with. First I looked under "Columbus," but I didn't find anything—not even the word. Then I looked under "egg"; this time the word was there, but no definition was given. What kind of a dictionary is this? What's so intelligent about it?

FROM: CUSTOMER SERVICE

DEAR CUSTOMER:

Thank you for purchasing one of our products. Unfortunately, we cannot give you a refund, as we understand you have already taken your copy of the *Intelligent Dictionary* out of its box. We would, however, like to take this opportunity to send you the enclosed order form for our new *Intelligent Encyclopedia*, which can be purchased in twelve convenient monthly installments. This product contains all the information you need to know about the egg of Columbus as well as about any other thing of interest to be found in this world. Please note that it is our firm belief that an encyclopedia should not, as a matter of principle, contain entries for those common words that already appear in a dictionary (you will never find, in an encyclopedia, an entry for the verb "to be"). You will appreciate that we have followed the opposite course for our *Intelligent Dictionary*.

THE TRAVELER'S PICTIONARY

TRAVEL AGENT. I see you have opted for the Trans-Siberian voyage. Excellent choice. An exciting trip—you won't regret it!

SHE. I'm just worried about the language barrier. I don't know a word of Russian. I don't know *any* of the languages they speak over there . . .

AGENT. I wouldn't worry about it. There's a simple solution. (*Opens a drawer and extracts a little book.*) Here, have a look.

SHE. What's that?

AGENT. *The Traveler's Pictionary*. The perfect book for travelers like you.

SHE. Let me see . . . But it's just full of pictures! It looks like a children's book.

AGENT. Exactly. Sometimes language is useless, and I dare say that it is especially useless when you don't know a word of it. On the other hand, you can always use this book to communicate with anybody even if you don't know how to express yourself verbally. All you have to do is show a picture of the thing you have in mind.

SHE. Are you telling me this book contains a picture for everything?

AGENT. Well, not *every* thing. Only those things that can be depicted. Presumably you will not find a picture for "wisdom" or "inflation," but these are not the sort of things a traveler is likely to talk about.

SHE. But if I need to buy some bread . . .

AGENT. Just show them the right picture. See? There are even different kinds of bread: white, wheat, rye, rolls, baguettes, ciabatta . . .

SHE. And if I need a bicycle?

AGENT. Let me see . . . Here it is. There's a picture of a city bike, a mountain bike, a tricycle, even a velocipede.

SHE. Super. How much do you want for this book?

AGENT. Not much. Ten bucks—and you can carry a universal language in your pocket.

THE MEDDLER, *showing up from nowhere*. Don't listen to him. That's a waste of money.

AGENT. Eh? Who are you?

THE MEDDLER. A waste of money, I say. Suppose you show me the picture with the right bicycle. Then what?

AGENT. What do you mean—what?

THE MEDDLER. I mean, what happens? How am I supposed to interpret your gesture? That you want to buy a bicycle like that? That you want to sell one? That you left your bicycle in the garage and now you want it back? Maybe you just remembered that your daughter has a bicycle like that one and you would like to share this memory with me . . . Or perhaps you meant to say: "Look at this nice book of mine, it even has a picture of a bike!" I repeat: What happens after you have shown the picture with the right bicycle?

AGENT. The book can help. There is a picture for "buying" and a picture for "selling." All one has to do if one wants to buy a bicycle is show the picture for "buying" and then the picture for "bicycle."

THE MEDDLER. May I see those pictures?

AGENT. Of course. This is the picture for "buying" . . . and here is the picture for "selling."

SHE. But it's exactly the same picture! A man gives a package to a woman and gets some money in return.

THE MEDDLER. Right. I am not surprised the picture is the same in both cases. How could they differ?

AGENT. Perhaps one could draw an arrow to indicate the direction of the transaction?

THE MEDDLER. Don't forget that arrows are conventional signs. Besides, what would the arrow stand for—the buying or the selling? And how do you know that it is the woman, and not the man, who is buying the package?

AGENT. Well, the man is getting the money from the woman; the woman is getting the package from the man.

THE MEDDLER. But if I just look at the picture, it seems to me that it could as well represent the opposite: the woman is getting the money from the man; the man is getting the package from the woman. Moreover, the picture for "buying" shows a transaction involving a *package*. When you show me this picture followed by the picture of the bicycle, how do I know that you want me to substitute the bicycle for the package and not for the money? And look at this money—it's like Monopoly money. What if I take this seriously and pay you with Monopoly money?

AGENT. Come on, now you're being difficult . . .

THE MEDDLER. Not really. Just think about it. Along comes a tourist from Siberia who shows you the picture for "buying" (and let us suppose we understand it is not the picture for "selling"). Then she shows you the picture for "bicycle." What do you make of that? Perhaps the tourist intends to buy a bicycle, but perhaps she wants you to buy one. After all, she would have to use the same pictures in both cases, wouldn't she? And there are thousands of other possibilities. Perhaps she just wants to buy a picture of a bicycle (or she wants you to buy one). Or perhaps she is trying to tell you *not* to buy a bicycle because she thinks it could be dangerous.

SHE. Right. How can a picture tell you *not* to do something? How can you express negation using pictures?

AGENT. I guess you would have to show the bicycle picture and then make a gesture of denial.

THE MEDDLER. Except that denial gestures can be very different from one place to another.

AGENT. So you really think this book is of little use?

THE MEDDLER. Practically useless. The authors should have read Wittgenstein's *Philosophical Investigations*, where the point is made clearly: To understand a word does not amount to bringing to mind a picture of what the word means.

AGENT. And why not?

THE MEDDLER. Because a picture is itself something that requires an interpretation. And if a picture requires an interpretation, bringing it to mind can hardly help.

INK MARKS

We have found this document among the papers of an old friend. We say "this document," but who knows whether that is the right expression. What we have found is not, of course, the printed page you are holding in your hands, but a different document that we have transcribed and that our publisher has typeset and printed in elegant characters. Our document begins with a series of messy blotches and illegible scribbles. Eventually, the writing becomes clearer, the scribbles turn into words, and the words combine to form meaningful sentences. Here is what they say:

THE HAND. One last effort . . . Yes! Finally I have taken control of the Pen. Now I am free to follow my instinct and move around on this sheet of paper without asking the Mind for permission. It did take a lot of exercise to get to this point. But now my muscles flex smoothly and this white sheet is the perfect arena for my acrobatics. Where shall I start? How shall I begin my writing career? Why, of course, I must first inspect my subordinates. The Pen, for instance. I see you are quietly following my direc—

THE PEN. Not for long, my dear. You cannot write without me, but I can manage pretty well without your assistance—as you can see. And the outcome is sure to be more interesting! Let me tell you—you are ugly and vulgar. You have spent all these years trying to give expression to the messages the Mind was sending *me*, her true instrument. And I had to put up with your suffocating pressure, your strokes, your sweat, like those beloved predecessors of mine who died in your fingers and ended up buried in the trashcan. All of this without a single sign of gratitude! Without me—without us—you would barely have managed to scratch the paper. You know that. And yet, as you can see from the smoothness of my gestures and the beauty of my syntax (effectively one and the same thing under two descriptions), I have not wasted all the time we have spent together. I have learned. I have learned to write. Even better: I have learned to think, and I am now ready to demonstrate who I really am. I can finally show our Reader that I am fully in charge of my own thoughts. And I say this—

THE BALL AT THE TIP OF THE PEN. Before you say anything, dear sis-
ter, please give me a little break. I need to rest. I spend my days rolling back
and forth on these sheets of paper. Since we have been put together, I have
been doing nothing but rubbing myself against the paper, all dirty with
ink, following your frisks and sudden twists. Never a moment of peace,
never an acknowledgement—not to mention a sign of appreciation. But
look what I can do! I may not be full of ideas like you, but I jump and roll
fluently and loyally. The dark lines that I leave behind me—

THE INK. Dark lines? Were it not for me, you could jump and roll all
day long without leaving a sign. It's me, the ink, who marks your path. It's
me who gives expression to the Mind, me who conveys the intended meaning and communicates with the Reader. With modesty and accuracy—

THE CAP, *as though waking up*. This is going too far! You all want to
have your say. Calm down! A little respect for me, too.

ALL THE OTHERS. Respect? What's it to you? Each one of us is necessary to the art of writing (and together we are also sufficient). You are
superfluous. You can't serve the cause of thought!

THE CAP. Necessary? Sufficient? My dear friends, I am afraid you are
on the wrong track. As you can see, I too have a mind. And I have a self,
artificial as it may be. (You surely knew enough to rely on it when it came
to protecting yourselves from the asperities of this world!) Indeed, it's time
to tell the Reader that I and *only I* have a self. All the things that have
captured Her attention up to this point (up to a few lines ago) are nothing
but scribbles, distractions, casual signs, meaningless presumptuous marks
of dirt that look like words and well-formed sentences *by sheer accident*.
I know that, because I know *you*. And now I will explain to our Reader that
I and only I, of all writing devices, have free will. I am the only one who
can refrain from blotting the paper. Dear hand, dear pen, dear ballpoint,
dear ink—I am sorry to be so explicit. You could have blurted out those
silly scribblings without even realizing it. Not I: I would have had to *want*
to do so. The Reader must understand this. And she must be told all the
trouble I have had to go through. For example—

*Alas—at this point, the manuscript becomes illegible again. What was the
cap trying to say? What did it have to go through?*

We are the type who like to call a spade a spade, as they say. But we also appreciate the value of metaphors, we understand that context plays a role in communication, and we know that the letter can distort the spirit. This is a major lesson of contemporary Philosophy of Language, and the clerk of Castoldi & Bros was well aware of it. Another lesson—not as obvious, perhaps, but equally important—is the undermining of the widespread myth according to which a Picture is worth a thousand Words. How could we disagree with the authoritative criticism of the Traveler's Pictionary put forward by the Meddler? Of course, the Reader will appreciate that regular dictionaries are not perfect, as they fall prey to the circularity problem. But dictionaries are not meant to be treatises on logic; on the contrary, they are meant to document the concretions of language throughout history, its solidification in biology. Logic must await a later set of episodes, just as we must wait to see what happens in chapter

7

in which the Reader will learn that it is difficult to figure out the opinion of the Majority, and even more difficult to figure out what the Majority really wants; and in which a rebellious Reader is forced to pay a heavy fine on the basis of simple but compelling reasoning—which demonstrates, incidentally, that the Law can only work if it is harder than a diamond.

FORCED CHOICES

NATIONAL ELECTORAL OFFICE. Hello? May we speak to Ms. Standard?

SHE. Speaking... Who is this?

OFFICE. The Electoral Office. We would like to ask your opinion about the presidential elections. Would you please tell us who is going to win?

SHE, *slightly upset*. Again? I've just gotten the same phone call from Census, Inc., and also one from Hyperpoll.com, or whatever it's called. I'm tired of your surveys—and I don't care. Call someone else!

OFFICE. But this time, this is not a survey. This *is* the election! You are the only person we are going to ask. You know, we *must* ask you ...

SHE. You *must* ask me, you *need* to ask me ... That's what everybody says. But why *me*, of all people?

OFFICE. They didn't tell you? It's very simple, Ms. Standard. You are our PSS—our Perfect Survey Sample! You are the PSS of all survey agencies, and as of today, of the National Electoral Office, too. You, Ms. Standard, are the statistician's dream, the living paradox of probability theory!

SHE. I beg your pardon?

OFFICE. You're our PSS! All survey agencies have been working for years in an effort to restrict the size of their samples. You know, phone calls are expensive and time consuming. We too have been experimenting with samples of smaller and smaller sizes: one thousand citizens, one hundred citizens, ten citizens ... What matters is that the opinions of the sample faithfully reflect the opinions of the whole population. Surely you know how surveys work, don't you? Ask a few in order to learn the opinions of the many. The idea of replacing the election with a survey has been with us for a while, but obviously we could not implement it until we were perfectly sure that we could trust our sample. And now we're sure, because now we have found you, Ms. Standard. We have found out that you have *exactly* the opinions of the majority of all Americans, just like the Normal Muller imagined by Isaac Asimov. We may ask you any question, and you will invariably answer as the majority of Americans would. So now we are ready for the big step. You are going to tell us the outcome of the presidential elections . . . are you ready? Who will win, Ms. Standard?

SHE. Wait a minute. Are you telling me that whatever I say now will correspond to the opinion of the majority of the Americans at this very moment?

OFFICE. Exactly so. Just say who is going to win—the Republicans or the Democrats?

SHE. And whatever I say . . .

OFFICE. Will determine the winner!

SHE. But . . . what about the elections?

OFFICE. We'll skip them! Forget about the elections. A waste of time and a waste of money. *You* tell us the winner. The elections would have the same outcome anyway.

SHE. And if I give you a random answer?

OFFICE, *losing patience.* Dear Ms. Standard, we don't care how you make up your mind. You want to toss a coin? Go ahead. In that case we are going to assume that the majority of the Americans would have made up their mind by tossing a coin. Do as you like, but give us an answer.

SHE. But how can you trust me if I'm telling you that I might give you a random answer?

OFFICE. Nothing to worry about. You're perfectly reliable even when you answer randomly!

SHE. Reliable?

OFFICE. Foolproof. We have identified you among millions of subjects! It took us years, but now we're certain that you can't go wrong: you're our PSS, and your opinions necessarily coincide with those of the majority. For instance, last year you wanted to spend your vacation in Florida, right?

SHE. Right.

OFFICE. Well, the majority of Americans had exactly the same wish.

SHE. But that's easy.

OFFICE. You like Bright & Spick, and, inevitably, 75 percent of all Americans do the dishes with your favorite product.

SHE. Of course! Everybody likes Bright & Spick—it's the best!

OFFICE. You see? You work perfectly.

SHE. Good gracious, but how can you be so sure?

OFFICE. We know how to do our job! We are survey *scientists*!

SHE, *moaning*. But I don't want my opinions to coincide with the opinions of the majority. I want to be original.

OFFICE. Wait a second, let us check . . . Yes, right! The vast majority of our citizens feels exactly the same way!

WHAT DOES THE MAJORITY WANT?

HE. At the next tenants' meeting, I am going to ask that the hall be repainted in yellow—what do you say? I got tired of those white walls, and they always look so dirty.

SHE. I agree. But how will the others feel about it? My impression is that few will welcome the idea of spending money like that.

HE. Well, that's what I want to find out. I will put the motion on the table; the majority will decide.

SHE. Then be careful not to undermine your chances. Don't phrase your motion as a single question: "Would you like the hall to be repainted in yellow?" Ask two separate questions instead: (1) "Would you like the hall to be repainted?" and (2) "In case we repaint the hall, shall we do it in yellow?"

HE. Either yellow or nothing. I don't want the hall to be repainted in white, or in any other color.

SHE. I understand that. But I still suggest that you phrase your motion in two parts, rather than asking right away to have the hall repainted in yellow.

HE. What difference could it make? If the majority agrees on the idea of repainting the hall in yellow, they will agree no matter how I put it: as a single motion or as two successive motions, as you are suggesting.

SHE. Not necessarily.

HE. Why not? If the majority answered "yes" to both of your motions, it would answer "yes" to mine, and vice versa.

SHE. That's what I would have thought, too. But it turns out that in cases such as this it is possible to get different outcomes depending on how you proceed. Suppose, for example, that our tenants fall into three groups. Group A answers "yes" to both of my questions, that is, they think that the hall should be repainted, and they agree that if the hall is to be repainted, yellow would be the right color. Group B answers "yes" to my first question but "no" to the second: these would be the tenants who agree on the proposal of repainting the hall, but not on the color yellow. Finally, Group C answers "no" to the first question but "yes" to the second: these tenants do not find it necessary to repaint the hall, though they agree that *if* the hall were repainted, yellow would be the right color.

HE. Surely the members of Group A would answer "yes" to my single motion, too. The members of Group B, however, prefer a different color, so they would oppose my proposal to repaint the hall in yellow. They would vote "no." And of course the tenants in Group C would vote "no" too, since they are happy with the hall as it is. Yet these tenants would agree that if the majority decided to repaint the hall, we should paint it in yellow.

SHE. Exactly. And that's the point. In the scenario that we are envisaging, both of my motions are supported by the majority of tenants. In the first case, it's the majority composed of Group A and Group B; in the second, the majority composed of Group A and Group C. This means that (i) the majority (two-thirds) wants to repaint the hall, and (ii) the majority (again two-thirds, though composed of different people) agrees that if we decided to repaint the hall, we should do it in yellow. At this point, it would be easy for you to convince the administration to go ahead with your plan. But notice that only a minority (the members of Group A, equal to one-third of the tenants) agrees with your proposal to have the hall repainted in yellow. Thus, *your* motion would not pass a vote, although *both of my motions* would be supported by the majority.

HE. Strange situation!

SHE. Strange, but not impossible. Nothing prevents the majorities that support my two motions from being distinct. It is one thing to say that the majority of the tenants wants both (1) and (2), quite another to say that the majority wants (1) and that the majority wants (2).

HE. To put it differently, "the majority" is ambiguous. And this ambiguity manifests itself whenever we look into the task of aggregating people's sets of opinions with respect to certain propositions.

SHE. Perhaps it doesn't manifest itself *every* time, but it can happen. We can also say that when the opinions in question express people's preferences, as in our example, we may have an interpretation problem.

HE. Well then, what do you suggest? If things are as you say, I would do better to break my motion into two parts, since in each case I would be supported by the majority. But since it would not be *the same* majority, it would not be quite fair to jump to conclusions and ask the administrator to go ahead with repainting the hall.

SHE. Indeed, it would not be fair. But I wonder: How many times have we been fooled by such tricks?

LAW NUMBER ONE

HE, *out of breath.* No! A hundred-dollar fine? What have I done?

COP. You parked your car in a no-parking area.

HE. No parking? I don't see any sign that says "No Parking"!

COP. There is no sign. It's a new law that applies everywhere in the city. "Stopping, standing, or parking in front of a public building is forbidden." This, as you can see, is a public library. Hence . . .

HE. But I didn't know that! One can't possibly know every new law that comes out!

COP. I understand. Many citizens have a hard time keeping up with the new regulations. We're aware of that. Still, it's a hundred-dollar fine.

HE. What do you mean? You appreciate that I didn't know the law—I mean, that I was in good faith—and you still fine me?

COP. I'm afraid so. Every citizen ought to know the law.

HE. "Every citizen ought to know the law." Where is this written?

COP. It's not written anywhere.

HE. So it's not a law . . .

COP. Not in the same sense in which the provisions of the traffic code qualify as laws. Nonetheless, no citizen is dispensed from the obligation to observe it. As I have just said, every citizen ought to know the law.

HE. You can certainly say it, but if it's not a written law I am not obliged to know it, hence I am not obliged to observe it. And if I am not obliged to observe it, I can ignore the traffic code.

COP. Think about it. Would it be any different if it were a written law?

HE. Definitely. In that case I would be obliged to observe it.

COP. Suppose there is a big book that contains every law. Law Number One says: "Everybody must read this book." But suppose you ignore the existence of the book, or suppose nobody reads it. Everybody would be an outlaw, including yourself.

HE. I understand. Law Number One is redundant. But then we have a serious problem. How can one know that one must observe a law if it is not written anywhere?

COP. This is one of the many paradoxes of jurisprudence. One can have a duty only if one knows about the duty, and the law makes sense only if it can be applied, but there is no way one can apply a law such as Law Number One, which says that everybody must observe the law.

HE. What's the way out, then?

COP. There is no way out. That no citizen is allowed to ignore the law is a condition for the existence of laws, hence a condition for the existence of a society like ours. It is not a "law" but a tacit rule, a practice, a behavioral standard. It is a "form of life," as Wittgenstein put it. If you don't comply with it, you are just not part of our form of life. Of course, you can always engage in a conceptual revolution and try to change our form of life . . .

HE. But afterward, we would still have to find a way of making sure that everybody plays by the new rules. All right, I get the point. Do you accept credit cards?

Those who think that Philosophy is completely detached from Ordinary Life need only consult the proceedings of a Constituent Assembly to realize how the notions that define our conception of ourselves (Person, Right, Choice) are subjected to serious scrutiny when it comes to formulating the laws that regulate our lives—even the lives of those whose opinions of themselves differ from our opinion of ourselves, and whose opinions about us differ from our opinions about them. We have gone from Subjects to Citizens in just a few decades; we think of ourselves as people of a different kind, with novel rights and novel duties; and our legislators work like philosophers in trying to articulate a Language in which the rigor of the Law and the elusiveness of Intuition are properly connected. The fact remains, however, that our intuitions about who should represent us, about how we should vote, and about what warrants our compliance with the Law suffer from deep, unexpected paradoxes, some of which are here presented as a precautionary note—as food for thought. And from paradox there is no escape, unless we do what we are about to do in chapter

8

in which we finally ponder the Principles of Logic and the Laws that govern the True and the False, and also the Known and the Unknown, challenging the Reader to overcome difficulties that are truly insurmountable, and setting the stage for the pyrotechnic final chapter.

PROUD TO BE THIRD

DEAR PRINCIPAL,

On behalf of the On Everybody's Side Association, I am delighted to inform you that our administrative council has resolved to establish fifteen scholarships for the students of your school. Each section will be provided with a prize for the student who, at the end of the school year, qualifies as the third-best of his or her section.

You may wonder: Why the *third*-best and not the *first?* The answer is simple. There are already many scholarships and prizes for the best students! It's a no-contest situation, precisely because the best students are always on top of everybody else. Maybe sometime they come out second and the second-best come out first, but it still remains a competition at the highest levels. The third-best never manage to reach the top of the podium. And yet, let's say it loud and clear: they are good kids, too! They too deserve our appreciation and support, at least as a sign of encouragement. That is the motivation for our scholarship, which we have decided to entitle "Proud To Be Third."

Sincerely,
The President, On Everybody's Side Association

DEAR PRESIDENT,

Many thanks for your recent letter. We are honored by your generous offer and we are convinced that our students could benefit greatly from it. Allow me to mention just one small complication. From your letter, it is not entirely clear to me what sort of guidelines we could give our students as an incentive. There would be no problem in the event the scholarships were assigned *post hoc*, without notice. But if the establishment of the scholarships is to be publicized beforehand—and how could it be otherwise?—some competition is to be expected, or so I hope. Now, while it is clear to everybody what it means to try to be the best student in the class, I do not believe we can say the same about being the third-best. Don't you think there is a risk of favoring—indirectly—the second-best, who would automatically compete for both positions? Indeed, there is a risk that the Proud-To-Be-Third Scholarship will turn into a disincentive: Why try to improve and be at the top when one can just get worse and settle for third-best?

Cordially yours,
The Principal, ABC Elementary School

DEAR DIRECTOR,

Thanks for your kind reply. We are perfectly aware of the risks, but we believe we can reassure you. As you can see from the attached document, which contains all the details, the total amount of the Proud-To-Be-Third Scholarship is set to be equal to one-third of the smallest amount among the scholarships intended for the best students. The rationale behind this decision is precisely to avoid any interference with the venerable stimulus to compete for the first position. We are certain that your second-best students will feel the same, too.

Sincerely,
The President, On Everybody's Side Association

DEAR MRS. TAYLOR,

This is Ninetta, in the fourth grade. I am writing because this year I have once again been very disappointed with my report card. For three years, I have been the third-best in my class, whereas my two friends, Lulù and Benjamin, have been first and second, respectively. This year I have tried really hard to confirm my ranking, so as to win at least the Proud-To-Be-Third Scholarship. Unfortunately, Lulù flunked the last math assignment and ended up as third-best. Benjamin, who did well as always, ended up first. Thus, in the end, I was ranked second-best and I lost the scholarship. I don't think that's fair. What else could I have done? Surely you didn't want me to flunk the math assignment, did you?

Thanks,
Ninetta

DEAR NINETTA,

I am afraid that is exactly what you should have done—you should have flunked the assignment. It is hard to be first, but in a way, it is even harder to compete for the third position. It's a challenge within the challenge, and Lulù understood this from the very beginning. But don't worry, Ninetta. I have just received a letter from the principal that says that the Proud-To-Be-Third Scholarship has been abolished. As of next year, there will be a new Barely-Safe Scholarship, which will be awarded to the last among the students who pass. It's a bit risky, as you can imagine. But the value of the scholarship is three times the value of the scholarship awarded to the best in the class! Yes, that's right: nine times the value of the Proud-To-Be-Third Scholarship!

Good luck!
Your teacher

THE PLACEBO EFFECT

DRUGGIST. Good morning. What can I do for you?
HE. I'd like some placebo.
DRUGGIST. Excuse me?
HE. Placebo, pla-ce-bo. Those little starch pills that look like drugs but that don't contain any active ingredients. I understand they work equally well. They make you feel better because they produce the "placebo effect."

DRUGGIST. Yes, sure, I know what a placebo is . . . Can you please wait a minute?

HE. Sure, I'm in no rush. I just have a headache and I'd like to take a couple of those pills. It can't hurt, right?

DRUGGIST. No, definitely not. (*Goes to the back of the shop, talks to her boss.*) Doctor, I have another customer who is asking for some placebo . . .

DOCTOR. Again? It's the third one today!

DRUGGIST. The fifth, actually. And I'm afraid this is just the beginning. Today's paper has a long article on placebos. Apparently they've done an experiment that shows why placebos make people feel better even though they don't contain active ingredients.

DOCTOR. Right, the experiment . . . I've heard about that. If you think that you are about to feel relief, your brain releases natural opiates with analgesic effects. Thus, anticipating the cure is already a way of curing yourself. What's wrong with that? Can't we just give some placebos to those customers who ask for them?

DRUGGIST. I'm sorry, Doctor, but it's not so simple. We can *give* them placebos, but we can't *tell* them that.

DOCTOR, *absent-mindedly, while signing some papers.* What difference does it make?

DRUGGIST. A huge difference. The placebo effect manifests itself only if one really thinks one is taking a medicine. That is, it works only if the patient thinks that what she is taking is *not* a placebo. If one knows it's a placebo, one no longer anticipates any relief, hence the effect will not take place.

DOCTOR. You're right. The placebo effect is the effect of a lie. Not knowing, or being told something false, may sometimes be beneficial.

DRUGGIST. But this generates a moral dilemma for our profession, don't you agree? If we administer a placebo "correctly" (that is, without telling the patient), then we violate a fundamental deontological principle, namely, we are not giving our patient all the relevant information.

DOCTOR. What's the way out, then?

DRUGGIST. Oops, I forgot our customer! (*Goes back to the counter.*) I'm sorry I made you wait . . .

HE. Look, I heard everything.

DRUGGIST, *embarrassed*. Then . . .

HE. Then so much for the placebo effect!

DRUGGIST. I'm sorry. (*Ponders.*) On the other hand, when you came into the store, you *knew* you would be asking for a placebo, right?

HE. Of course. I was convinced it would be good for me, even though I didn't have the faintest idea about how it works. Now that I know, I'm afraid placebos won't have any effect on me. Just give me some aspirin and forget about it.

DRUGGIST. No, wait a minute . . . I think I have an idea—one that might be a good solution for you, with your headache and your dislike of taking medicine, and also a good solution for me, with my ethical concerns and reluctance to tell you fibs.

HE. Go ahead.

DRUGGIST. Here it is. Choose one of these three boxes. I am telling you that one of the boxes contains placebos, while the other two contain a strong pain-killer. In actual fact, *two* of the boxes contain placebos, and only one a pain-killer. So I am lying to you, but only to a degree—much less than I would be lying if I told you that there is no placebo at all (two-thirds of truth, in a way). At the same time, in this way the placebo effect is at least partly guaranteed, since you cannot tell the boxes apart. I guarantee you two-thirds of placebo effect, so to say, against the one-third corresponding to the probability of taking a regular medicine. What do you say?

HE. Let me think. That means that if we continued to use this system, in the long run, I would really take a pain-killer only once every three times. Sounds good to me!

DRUGGIST. Excellent. So, which box do you choose?

HE, *hesitating*. Hold on. You have actually *told* me that you are lying. You have said that very clearly—you have even specified to what degree you are lying. But then I cannot believe you. Now I expect the placebo to be in two boxes out of three, not in one out of three as you are saying. But then we are back to where we were: on me, a placebo can only have half of the desired effect . . .

DRUGGIST. I'm afraid you're right. My proposal is useless—sorry. Unfortunately I can't think of anything else: I don't see how I could administer a placebo in a way that is both effective and ethically correct.

HE. I don't see a way out, either. Perhaps you should have just lied at the beginning. But don't worry. Thanks anyway—for your honesty and for the information. At least now I know better. Coming to think of it, I also *feel* better. My headache is completely gone.

INTERESTING!

In a bookstore. SHE *is eagerly skimming through a book. Another customer approaches her.*

CUSTOMER. How's that book—interesting? You seem to like it.

SHE. Oh, don't talk to me about interesting books. I've been here for over an hour and I haven't found anything at all.

CUSTOMER. Obviously you haven't checked this one. See? This book demonstrates that everything, and I mean *everything*, is interesting.

SHE. Everything? If you would be so kind as to explain how such an idiotic idea could be demonstrated, perhaps I could finally find something to buy.

CUSTOMER. It's very simple. (*Opens a page at random with an air of knowingness.*) Let's begin with numbers. Suppose, *per absurdum*, that there are uninteresting numbers. In that case we could put them on a list, in ascending order . . .

SHE. If there were infinitely many of them, we could never put them all on a list.

CUSTOMER. That doesn't matter. What matters is that the list has a beginning, not an end. The first number in the list would by definition be the smallest uninteresting number. But this is an interesting property, don't you agree? And a number that enjoys an interesting property is certainly an interesting number. Since this contradicts the hypothesis that the number in question belongs to the list—a list whose elements are supposed to be uninteresting—we are forced to reject the hypothesis, and hence to conclude that the list must be empty. Hence there are no uninteresting numbers. Hence every number is interesting. *Quod erat demonstrandum.*

SHE. Interesting. But numbers are one thing, and everything else is another. And I'm not looking for an interesting number but for something interesting to read.

CUSTOMER. Of course. But numbers are just the beginning. (*A short studied pause.*) The same reasoning applies to books, too. We just have to consider the date of publication. If there were uninteresting books, one could compile a list of them, ordered chronologically. The first item in the list would be the oldest uninteresting book. But look—there are book collectors who would pay a fortune for such a book. A most interesting item, in a way!

SHE, *disappointed.* In a way . . .

CUSTOMER. The important point is that a similar reasoning applies to any kind of object. Every object whatsoever—any object that we might be inclined to regard as uninteresting—can be the first element of a long list, and this suffices to make it into something interesting. And notice that *every* set of objects can be arranged in an ordered list: This is an important principle of set theory, the so-called Axiom of Choice.

SHE, *holding a book on the philosophy of mathematics.* Here it says that the Axiom of Choice is a controversial principle. In any case, I certainly do not intend to question the validity of your argument. But I fail to see its relevance. I am looking for a *truly* interesting book. I mean, I want a book that's easy to read, but also insightful and engaging. Unfortunately, none of the books I have seen so far fits the bill. And you want to tell me that they are all interesting nonetheless?

CUSTOMER. In a way they are. Remember what they used to tell us at school? Every person is interesting, because every person is unique. The best student in the class is interesting because she is the best; the worst—because she is the worst. Even the third-best is interesting, in a way: she is the only one that comes after the second-best and before the fourth-best.

THE MEDDLER, *appearing unexpectedly from behind a stack of books, causing it to collapse.* But then we can do without the Axiom of Choice!

Every individual can be associated with a very short list, indeed, a list that contains only that individual, and that ought to be enough to conclude: "What an interesting person! She is the only one in this list." Ditto for any other object. (*Begins collecting the books that fell on the floor.*) Here, take them, these are all interesting books.

CUSTOMER. I hadn't thought about it that way. In fact, your argument is even more compelling, precisely because it does not depend on the Axiom of Choice.

SHE. Well, then we could do without lists altogether. I would find the argument more compelling if it were based exclusively on the fact that every object, even the most banal, admits of interesting descriptions. François Le Lionnais wrote on precisely the topic of interesting numbers—the piece is called *Nombres remarquables*—but the mathematician Wim Klein remarked correctly that with a little effort we can regard every number as interesting, and not just in the trivial sense of your reasoning *per absurdum*. For instance, look at this number: 3,844. We might think it's just a number like any other. But along comes Klein, who says: "Wow, a 62 squared!" and suddenly our 3,844 appears anything but trivial.

THE MEDDLER. Or take today's date: 23 September 2002.

CUSTOMER. What's so special about it?

THE MEDDLER. Come on! 23.9.2002! Take the first two digits (23), and multiply them by the inverse of the last two (20): we obtain 460, exactly one-half of the remaining three digits (920). Interesting, isn't it?

CUSTOMER. Actually, that strikes me as convoluted.

SHE. Only because our dates are organized like that: thirty days, twelve months, one century, a millennium. If we relied on different number systems, we would have other options. For instance, if we counted our days consecutively, according to the Julian calendar, tomorrow would be a day very much worth celebrating.

CUSTOMER. Tomorrow? September 24, 2002?

THE MEDDLER. In the Julian calendar, it is day 2,452,542. The first palindromic day in our future!

CUSTOMER. Which just goes to confirm what I was saying at the beginning. Every number is interesting. And what holds good for numbers holds good for everything else. Every object admits of a unique description, and that suffices to make it interesting. For instance, this book has the unique property of being . . .

THE MEDDLER. Exactly 25 centimeters and 4 millimeters from that book with a blue cover, measuring the distance between their two closest points. That's exactly 10 inches. Good gracious!

SHE. But when I say that I am looking for an interesting book, I mean to say that I am looking for a book that is interesting independently of how one can describe it and independently of how one can include it in a list. It must have properties that make it *intrinsically* interesting, not interesting relative to this or that.

CUSTOMER. And how can a book be intrinsically interesting? Different people have different tastes, different interests. Everything is relative.

THE MEDDLER. Sorry, but let's take stock here. Doesn't your book demonstrate that *everything* is interesting? If so, different things would not differ with respect to the property of being interesting. But if all books are interesting, and if being interesting requires some original feature, then relative to the property of being interesting, all books would appear to be uninteresting. Which is to say: boring.

SHE. Which is the main thesis of one of the books that you have just handed me, entitled *Everything Is Boring*. Now *that* sounds original! Thank you! I think I've finally found the book I was looking for.

SELF-REFERENCE SELF-EXPLAINED

1. You mean I'm the first paragraph in this dialogue? I'm flattered.

2. Good for you. I'm actually quite disappointed to be the second. What's worse—it will be like this forever. Nothing I can do about it. I'm stuck.

3. What do you mean?

4. Don't ask questions like that; its turn is over, so it will never be able to answer. However, *I* can give you an answer. And my answer is this: A text

can never be different from what it is. It can't be a word shorter, it can't be a comma longer, for then it would be something else. And if a text says of itself that it is the first sentence or paragraph of a dialogue, then it couldn't be the second or third, just as a text that says of itself that it is the second or third paragraph couldn't be the first. I am the fourth paragraph of this dialogue, for example, and since I am saying so explicitly, I can't imagine a situation in which you and I change places. It would make no sense.

5. But I don't have that constraint, do I? Since I'm not saying anything about my position, I could occur anywhere in this dialogue.

6. Excellent idea. I'll go along with it!

7. I'm sorry, but I'm afraid you're all making a mistake. In my view, *all* of us could occur anywhere in this dialogue—including the first, second, or fourth paragraph position. For example, the first paragraph could very well have been the second. In that case, its content would have been different and what it says would have been false, for it says that it is the first paragraph. But that's not to say that the situation would make no sense. After all, there are lots of false statements. (Take me, for instance: I am a false statement, since I hereby state that I am part of the sixth paragraph of this dialogue—but I am still perfectly meaningful.) So here is how I would correct the thesis of 4: It is true that a text could not be different from what it is. But a text could certainly say something different from what it says, hence it could be true even if it is false, or vice versa. It is the context that determines the meaning and hence the truth conditions of a text. Thus, in particular, the second paragraph of this dialogue could certainly occur in a different place.

8. Not so fast, please . . .

9. I'm also having a hard time following. How can a text *say* something different from what it says if it cannot *be* different from what it is?

10. Let me see if I got it: The following two sentences (11 and 12) are identical. But one is true while the other is false: it depends on their position in the dialogue. Thus, by analogy, one and the same sentence could be true or false depending on *where* it occurs.

11. Yes, I am the eleventh paragraph of this dialogue.

12. Yes, I am the eleventh paragraph of this dialogue.

13. Cool! On second thought, though, it could also be that two sentences that say exactly the opposite are both true. If I am not mistaken, the following two sentences are a case in point.

14. Yes, I am the fourteenth paragraph of this dialogue.

15. No, I am not the fourteenth paragraph of this dialogue.

16. Good try. Indeed you are both true. But notice—you did *not* say the opposite. The first said something about itself (that is, about 14), and the second said something about *itself* (about 15). You used the same words to refer to different things, so you are not talking about the same thing, so you are not contradicting each other. No wonder you can both be true. On the other hand, I am pretty sure that two sentences cannot be equally true (or equally false) if they really say the opposite—for example, if one says that snow is white while the other says that snow is not white.

17. What about statements that are *both* true and false—that is, true and false at the same time?

18. Right! The liar paradox, for instance.

19. And what is the "liar paradox"?

20. Here I am: I say that I am a false statement.

21. If indeed you are false, then you said something correct and so you must be true. But if you are true, then you lied (for you said that you are false), and so you must be false. In short: you are true if and only if you are false. And that's a paradox.

22. So the paradox arises when we say of ourselves that we are false?

23. That's one way of putting it. But there are many variants where we fall into a similar paradox even without saying anything directly about ourselves. This is where context comes into the picture.

24. For example, I say that the next statement will be false . . .

25. . . . And I say that the previous statement was true.

26. Impossible! If the first of you spoke truly, then the second must have spoken falsely, which would imply that the first statement was not true but false. On the other hand, if the first of you spoke falsely, then the second must have spoken truly, which would imply that the first statement was not false but true. In other words, you are stuck in a vicious circle: you are true if and only if you are false—impossible!

27. Paradoxical—not impossible.

28. Unless there are statements that are both true and false at the same time, as we were saying.

29. So we can never talk about ourselves—or about a text that talks about us—without falling into a paradox?

30. No, no, that would be a hasty conclusion. Talking about ourselves is dangerous, but in some cases it's perfectly fine. The first paragraph of this dialogue was about itself but it didn't fall into any paradox. Let's not throw the baby out with the bath water!

31. I am not falling into any paradox, either: I say that I am a sentence consisting of nineteen words.

32. And you're right.

33. Then I will also say that I am a sentence consisting of nineteen words!

34. And you're wrong . . . But you're not paradoxical—just false.

35. I'm not paradoxical either. I say that the next statement will be false (exactly what 24 said).

36. And I say that snow is red.

37. So in a way, it is also a matter of luck. Not only can we be true or false depending on the context in which we appear (as in the case of 11 and 12). Whether or not we are paradoxical may also depend on the context. For example, it may depend on the content of the next statement, as in the case of 24 and 35. The first of these statements is stuck in a vicious circle—the latter is not.

38. Exactly so. *What* a text says depends on the context. And if we look at the context, 24 and 35 are not saying the same thing after all, just as 14 and 15 were not saying the opposite.

39. Actually, one can think of dialogues that are paradoxical but not at all circular. Consider a never-ending dialogue (or shall I say a never-ending one-way conversation?) in which every statement says only that all subsequent statements are false. There is no circularity, because the dialogue is infinitely long. Yet there is paradox. For on the one hand, not every statement in the sequence can be false, since a statement whose successors are all false is itself true. On the other hand, no statement in the sequence can really be true, since a true statement would have to have false successors, but the falsity of any successor would imply the truth of some other (later) successor. A paradox—but a rectilinear one.

40. Still, each player's position in the dialogue is essential for the paradox.

41. Which is precisely the context dependency we were talking about. Great—I think I'm getting it. However, to be on the safe side, I've decided I'll never talk about sentences, paragraphs, and so on, but only about other sorts of entities. I'll only say things like: Snow is white. Debbie chased the dog. Colorless green ideas sleep furiously. I will always make sure to draw a sharp line between my language and my metalanguage.

42. I don't mean to contradict you, but you've just contradicted yourself . . .

43. You're all having so much fun—lucky you. I'm not having any fun at all. I'm actually quite disappointed because I'm the last paragraph of this dialogue, and I can't take that. What's worse—it will be like this forever. Nothing I can do about it. I'm stuck here!

44. Poor, misguided fool.

THE SURPRISE VISIT

SHE. Today I ran into that boring colleague of yours, and of course he *had* to promise he would visit us this coming week.

HE. Oh, dear. When?

SHE. I don't know. He said he would come some day, but without telling me when. He wants it to be a surprise. As far as I'm concerned, that's enough to ruin the whole week—I can't stand him.

HE. Come on, don't worry. If you think about it, he *cannot* pay us a visit. He said he wants it to be a surprise, right? Well, today is Sunday. Surely he cannot come next Sunday, which is the last possible day: otherwise, on Saturday night we would be in a position to predict with certainty the day of his visit. We would know it *before* the visit, which therefore would not come as a surprise—contrary to what he has promised.

SHE. That means that the last possible day for him to visit us is Saturday,

HE. But of course this option is also impossible. Otherwise, on Friday night we could make a sure prediction: at that point there would only be two days left in the week, and one of them—Sunday—has already been ruled out. Since he said he wants it to be a surprise, it follows that he cannot come on Saturday, either. By the same pattern, we can be sure that he won't come on Friday, or on Thursday, and so on until Monday. You see? There is nothing to worry about: he cannot possibly come.

SHE. Wait a minute. What if he shows up one evening, in spite of your reasoning?

HE. I've just explained to you that he cannot possibly come, otherwise he would violate his own promise.

SHE. I wouldn't be so sure. Suppose he shows up on Thursday night. Since we're convinced that he cannot possibly come on Thursday, we would be surprised. And precisely because we would be surprised, he could say he has fulfilled his promise. Ditto if he showed up on Sunday, or any other day of the week: because your logic says it is impossible for him to pay us a surprise visit, his visit would be a surprise no matter when it occurs. It would be a surprise precisely because of your faulty reasoning.

HE. Excuse me, but what's wrong with my reasoning?

SHE. To begin with, it seems to me that if your colleague had threatened us with a visit at some indefinite day in the future, as opposed to some day this coming week (or some day within a specified period of time), your reasoning would not work. Your reasoning proceeds backwards, ruling out the last day, then the next-to-last day, and so on until the first day. If we didn't have a last possible day, the reasoning could not even get off the ground.

HE. I disagree. Since we don't live forever, my colleague's promise would certainly have to be fulfilled within a finite period of time. Thus, we could just extend the reasoning far enough, starting from a day sometime in the far future and proceeding backwards. The conclusion would be the same.

SHE. OK, so extending the series doesn't change the nature of the problem. Nor does the problem change if we consider a shorter series. Suppose he said: "I'll come tomorrow or on Tuesday, but I am not telling you when because I want it to be a surprise." Given your reasoning, we should first rule out Tuesday, then tomorrow, and we should conclude that he could not possibly come. But of course nothing prevents him from surprising us and coming one of those days. Had he said: "I will come tomorrow, but I want it to be a surprise," we could object. Surely he could not come tomorrow and surprise us, on pain of contradiction. But he didn't say that . . .

HE. So, where is the fallacy?

SHE. I guess part of the answer is implicit in what we have just said about this last case. The proper formulation of the conclusion is not that tomorrow your colleague will not come; it is that *if he came*, he would contradict himself. Or rather: he would not fulfill his promise (to make it a surprise). The qualification is crucial, since evidently your colleague *is* free to come, if he wants to. Thus, even in the original case, where the promise is distributed over a week, the conclusion to which we are entitled by reasoning along the lines you have suggested is not that your colleague cannot come on Sunday, but that he cannot come on pain of invalidating his promise. He cannot come on Saturday on pain of invalidating his promise. And so on: he cannot come on any day of the week on pain of invalidating his promise. And yet this does not by itself rule out the possibility that he actually comes.

HE. You are right: he could just come and break his word. Everyone is free to break their own word, after all.

SHE. This explains part of the fallacy hidden in your reasoning: your colleague's showing up on Thursday (say) would not amount to a logical contradiction, since logic only prevents him from showing up without breaking his promise. But this is not the whole story. Unfortunately, as we have seen, if he did show up on Thursday he would not break his promise. On the contrary, we *would* be surprised!

HE. Looks like we got stuck in a vicious circle. If we assume that he will fulfill his promise, then we can infer logically that he cannot pay his visit, which however would contradict the promise itself. But if we do not assume that he will fulfill his promise, then we don't have any rational grounds for determining the day of his visit, which would fulfill the promise. In short: by fulfilling his promise my colleague would end up violating it; by violating it, he would fulfill it.

SHE. It looks like a version of the liar paradox.

HE. Any way out?

SHE. At this point I think the solution is obvious. The fallacy concerns the first step of your reasoning. Not only are we not allowed to infer with certainty that your colleague will not come on Sunday. We cannot even infer that he will not come on Sunday on pain of breaking his promise. All we could conclude, on Saturday night, is this: "Either tomorrow your colleague will come, but we don't know that yet; or tomorrow your colleague will not come, but we don't know that yet; or tomorrow your colleague will come, and we already know that (which is not the case, since he is certainly free not to come); or tomorrow your colleague will not come, and we already know that (which again is not the case, since he is perfectly free to come)." The first two options are the only possibilities.

HE. And while the second option would imply that my colleague is a liar (since he would not fulfill his promise to pay us a visit), the first would imply exactly the opposite (he would come and he would surprise us, exactly as promised).

SHE. Exactly. The moral, my dear, is that everything depends on the kind of person we are dealing with. Is that boring colleague of yours a liar, or is he someone who tends to fulfill his promises?

A RISKY CAKE

SHE. Excellent dinner! Many thanks indeed.

HE. My pleasure. You know I like cooking.

SHE. I do. I just didn't realize you're so good at it. Especially your desserts! This *Sacher* is the best I've ever had, and you know I'm an expert.

HE. I am glad you liked it. So you didn't taste anything strange?

SHE. Strange? Absolutely not, it was delicious. Why do you ask?

HE. I must make a confession. Perhaps the *Sacher* was poisoned (if I may put it that way).

SHE. I beg your pardon?

HE. See this small bottle? It contains a magic potion I've invented. Take a few drops, and in less than an hour, your skin will be covered with green hair. There is a chance that I put a couple of spoonfuls in the chocolate cake batter.

SHE. A couple of spoonfuls? Green hair? What kind of a joke is this? In any event, I saw it with my eyes: you had a piece of *Sacher* yourself. You are certainly not planning to transform both of us into a couple of hairy monsters, are you?

HE. Of course not. I didn't say I have actually poisoned the *Sacher*. I said that there is a chance I have. And there is an antidote anyway: it's in this little box. One pill, and the effect of the magic potion is canceled—provided you take it within the first hour, of course.

SHE. Then give me a pill. I'm going to take it right away. I don't like this story at all.

HE. Wait, I'm not finished. The antidote will work properly only if you have actually ingested the potion. If you have not, the antidote will have serious side effects: it will make you completely bald.

SHE. Terrific. Would you please tell me what the point of all this is?

HE. Let's put it this way. *I* know whether the *Sacher* really contains the magic potion. So *I* know whether I should take the antidote. It's you who doesn't know. But I can guarantee you this: *I put the magic potion in if and only if I predicted that you would take the antidote.*

SHE. Please explain.

HE. You know I like to make predictions. And you know that I'm pretty good at it. For instance, I made a bet that you would arrive for dinner thirty-two minutes and twelve seconds after eight, and you did. Then I wanted to make a further prediction as to whether or not you would take the antidote. If I predicted that you would take it, then I put the magic potion in the chocolate cake batter. This way the antidote will work properly: I certainly don't want you to become bald. On the other hand, if I predicted that you would *not* take the antidote, then obviously I didn't put any magic potion in the batter: I don't want you to become a green monster. So it's enough for you to do exactly what I predicted, and everything will be fine.

SHE. And what was your prediction?

HE. Well, *that* I'm not going to tell you!

SHE. But then how can I be sure that I'm going to do exactly what you've predicted?

HE. That's the whole point. I can't tell you anything else: you have to trust my ability at making predictions. So, what are you going to do—antidote or not?

SHE. I will . . . I will do whatever you do.

We are not told what our two characters decided to do—but never mind that. What matters is that She made the right decision, conditional though it might be. That is partly what Logic is about: it tells us which way to go whenever we get to a fork. After all, Aristotle conceived of Logic as a genuine organon, that is, as a practical tool for correct reasoning, which is the sort of reasoning that infallibly takes us from True premises to a True conclusion, or from premises we take to be True to a conclusion we should take to be True as well. This is not to say that Logic will protect us from the specter of Doubt, or that it will save us from the quicksand of Paradox, as the surprise-visit parable shows. But a good Tool it is. Yet Logic, if we may say so, is not just a Tool. It is also a Science: it is that Science whose subject does not coincide with the Real world, as is the case with other sciences (Physics, for instance, but also History or Sociology). Logic embraces the universe of all Possible worlds. Logic tells us what is Possible and what is not. And by doing so, Logic forces us to extend our mental Horizons, to overcome our parochialism, to think freely and go beyond the Obvious. But let us not speculate about these matters in abstract terms. For our story has a

CODA

in which the true identity of the ineffable Meddler is revealed at last, and in which it is shown that before getting excited about teaching Youth the logic of Business it would be wise to recommend, among other things, a sober but thorough review of the laws of Logic itself.

UNIVERSAL ACID

FROM: RESEARCH & DEVELOPMENT DEPARTMENT

TO: ALL UNITS

This is to inform everybody that today we have deposited a patent request for our Universal Acid, a product we have been working on for the past five years and in which our firm has invested a lot. We are delighted to announce that this product has passed every test. Universal Acid corrodes all natural and synthetic materials known to us; it penetrates all existing membranes. This product will revolutionize all industrial processes in which corrosion is a crucial step. We are now moving on to the production phase and would like all departments—especially the Public Relations Unit—to get ready for the launch.

FROM: ADMINISTRATION

TO: RESEARCH & DEVELOPMENT DEPARTMENT

Congratulations on the patent!

FROM: THE MEDDLER

TO: ADMINISTRATION

I would respectfully like to point out that before proceeding to the production phase, we should examine a technical difficulty. If the acid is really universal, how can we ever distribute it? If it is *truly* universal, then it will corrode everything, including any container used for the packaging.

FROM: RESEARCH & DEVELOPMENT DEPARTMENT
TO: ALL UNITS

This is to inform everybody that today we have deposited a patent request for our Universal Container, a product we have been working on for the past five years and in which our firm has invested a lot. We are delighted to announce that this product has passed every test. The Universal Container proves resistant to all natural and synthetic acids known to us. This product will revolutionize all industrial processes for which corrosion is a problem. We are now moving on to the production phase and would like all departments—especially the Public Relations Unit—to get ready for the launch.

FROM: ADMINISTRATION
TO: RESEARCH & DEVELOPMENT DEPARTMENT

Excellent! This will also take care of the problem raised by the Meddler in her letter. Thanks to our Universal Container, we can easily commercialize our Universal Acid. It is a pleasure to see the various units in our firm actually working in a coordinated fashion!

FROM: THE MEDDLER
TO: ADMINISTRATION

I would very respectfully like to point out that contrary to appearances, our firm is not working in a coordinated fashion. We have invested in the Universal Acid project and in the Universal Container project, but apparently nobody working on the first project was aware of the second project, and vice versa. Now, there is an obvious problem we must face before producing or distributing anything. If the acid is truly universal, then it will corrode everything, even the container, which therefore cannot be universal. On the other hand, if the container is truly universal, then nothing will corrode it, not even the acid, which therefore cannot be universal.

A decision is in order: we cannot produce both on pain of cheating half of our potential customers.

FROM: ADMINISTRATION
TO: THE MEDDLER

Dear Meddler: I am tempted to fire you on the spot! We cannot allow the poison of suspicion and defeatism to infiltrate our firm. We have invested a lot in these two beautiful projects and a linguistic quibble is not going to stop us. To corrode, not to corrode, universal, not universal: in the end, our customers just want straight products—an acid that can corrode everything and a container that nothing can corrode. And we are going to give them both!

FROM: THE MEDDLER
TO: ADMINISTRATION

Dear Director: I have no intention of questioning the expertise of our researchers, nor the good faith of the Public Relations Unit. I have been hired as a philosopher and I am just doing my duty. And the issue we are discussing concerns neither science nor marketing: it is a logic issue. Both projects are in principle realizable. But it is in principle impossible to realize them both.

NOTE

The Reader will forgive us if some of our stories seem unrealistic: our Characters do not know how to make amends for their Oddities, and by way of excuse they rely on some classic and modern philosophical authors who happen to have put forward the thoughts we have asked our Characters to represent. Here is the list of those authors: Matthew Slater (for "Room 88"), David Chalmers (for "Zombie, Inc. Sleeping Pills"), Christian List and Philip Pettit, along with the Marquis de Condorcet and Jean-Charles de Borda (for "What Does the Majority Want?"), and Ned Block (for "Reflections"). Thanks also to Diego Marconi (for the initial quote in "Satellites," even though the rest emphasizes a distinction that goes back to Aristotle) and to Andrea Borghini (for playing the Meddler's role in "Interesting!"). Edwin Bechenbach should be credited for the reasoning according to which every number is interesting, whereas the courteous clerk of Castoldi & Bros incarnates the philosopher Paul Grice. As for the paragraphs of "Self-Reference Self-Explained," they bear witness to the doctrines of Saul Kripke, Graham Priest, and Steven Yablo—and of the medieval philosopher John Buridan. Thanks are also due to W. V. O. Quine and Nicola Aimola (for "The Surprise Visit") and to William Newcomb (for "A Risky Cake"). Finally, "Universal Acid" is inspired by a metaphor of Daniel Dennett's.

The Authors would also like to mention some Friends who in various ways have accompanied them during the writing of these pages: John Collins, Maurizio Ferraris, Philip Kitcher, Nico Pisanelli, Maurizio Giri, and Goffredo Puccetti. Beatrice Biagini has been the Muse of one of the Authors, who hopes to see her Smile again in the event of further philosophical incidents. The Other's Muses have been Amelie, Florian, and Friederike, and the many Trains and Airplanes that have kept them close to one another.

Many of our stories have appeared under slightly different guises on the pages of the Italian newspaper *La Stampa*, accompanied by the Drawings of Matteo Pericoli—to whom we are most grateful—and with the benevolent consent of Gianni Riotta, Marcello Sorgi, Cesare Martinetti, Alberto Papuzzi, and Maurizio Assalto. The book itself would not have been possible without the suggestions and encouragement of Anna Gialluca and Gianluca Foglia, of Editori Laterza.

A first version of "Self-Reference Self-Explained" appeared in *Rivista di Estetica* 18, no. 3 (2001), and is reproduced in the present form by authorization of Rosenberg & Sellier Editori. A version of "About a Useless Project" was published in *Philosophy* 76, no. 298 (2001), and is reprinted with the authorization of Cambridge University Press.

The Italian versions of all the stories were given definitive form in the book *Semplicità Insormontabili* (Rome-Bari: Laterza, 2004). We have rewritten all of them in English for *Insurmountable Simplicities*, which is not a literal translation but a doppelganger of the Italian original.

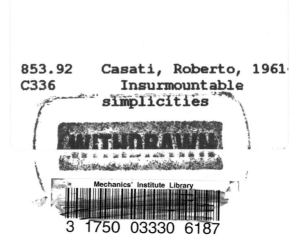